The Total Horse Barn Management *Makeover*

Practical Business Wisdom for Running Your Horse Business

By

Sheri Grunska

"A successful horse business is about so much more than great horse care. It's very much about the Owner/Client business relationship and how you handle the easy days and the tough days that are part of owning a horse business."

The Total Horse Barn Management *Makeover*

By

Sheri Grunska

Text Copyright 2015 © Sheri L. Grunska

All Rights Reserved

Learn more about the daily life of running a horse business
on my blog and website

www.probarnmanagement.com

Disclaimer

The purpose of this book is to acquaint the reader with horse barn management through the experience of the author. The information is drawn from the author's extensive experience owning and operating a horse business.

It is not all-inclusive, however, and is not intended to cover all circumstances or every situation which may arise. The author does not make any representations or warranties, either expressed or implied, regarding the techniques discussed and assumes no liability therefore.

Dedication

I want to thank my husband David who has been by my side every day for the last twenty-five years. Thank you for your constant support and always taking up the slack when I get something in my head and won't stop until it is done (like this book). You are my rock and I am blessed to walk through this life with you.

Acknowledgments

I want to thank some very wonderful people who edited this book for me. A huge thank you goes out to Bobbie Schmidt, Martha Schultz and Jon Richey for proof reading and editing. As I have found out in the past I am a terrible editor so I truly appreciate all the hours of work you put into this book. The photo credit for the cover goes to Carol Capener. Thank you for doing the impossible with someone who is not photogenic at all. I also want to thank Kari Navis for all your professional advice and encouragement. It truly does take a team to get a book published and I am so very blessed to have wonderful people working by my side to get this book done. Thank you from the bottom of my heart!

Table of Contents

Disclaimer 5

Dedication 6

Acknowledgments 6

The Reason I Wrote This Book 14

About This Book 15

Chapter 1 18

Open for Business. Are You Ready? 18

Chapter 2 21

What Barn Management is to Most People 21

Chapter 3 26

Let's Start With the Easy Part-The Barn Chores 26

Chapter 4 29

Stall Cleaning and Bedding 29

Chapter 5 33

Hay, Grain and Supplements 33

Chapter 6 45

Open Seven Days a Week 45

Chapter 7 48

Horses and Weather and the Many Different Opinions 48

Chapter 8 54

Not Enough Paddocks is a Problem 54

Chapter 9 58

What Is Included In Your Job Description as Barn Owner or Barn Manager? 58

Chapter 10 61

The Many Hats You Will Wear as the Barn Owner 61

Chapter 11 67
Fear Can Be the Big Reason Your Barn is Having So Many Problems 67
Chapter 12 70
Why Do So Many Horse Boarding Barns Go Out of Business? . 70
Chapter 13 73
Growing Pains of a New Business 73
Chapter 14 79
The Many Changes You Will Make in the Early Years 79
Chapter 15 84
It's a Working Farm 84
Chapter 16 87
Is Your Barn Designed for Horses or People? 87
Chapter 17 91
Barn Hours Are Important! 91
Chapter 18 95
Private Turnout vs. Group Turnout 95
Chapter 19 101
The Multi-Discipline Barn 101
Chapter 20 106
Renting and Sub-Leasing Your Stalls 106
Chapter 21 111
Has Your Tack Room Become Too Small? 111
Chapter 22 114
When a Horse Needs To Be Put Down 114
Chapter 23 118
The Challenges of Outdoor Board 118

Chapter 24 128

When Your Client and You Don't Agree 128

Chapter 25 132

Handling a Boarders Difficult Horse 132

Chapter 26 138

When Things Get Broken, Who Pays? 138

Chapter 27 141

Are You Prepared For Special Requests? 141

Chapter 28 145

Veterinarian's, Farriers and You the Barn Owner 145

Chapter 29 154

What Do You Offer With "Full Service" Board? 154

Chapter 30 157

Are Your Boarding Rates Too Low? 157

Chapter 31 160

The Issue Is Not Whether You Allow Back Shoes or Not 160

Chapter 32 164

Do You Have High Turnover At Your Barn? 164

Chapter 33 169

Trainers at Your Barn 169

Chapter 34 174

Employees 174

Chapter 35 181

Happy To Say "Yes" But Learn To Say "No" 181

Chapter 36 184

Do Your Boarders Understand the Barn Rules and Why You Have Them? 184

Chapter 37..205

Is Your Barn Set Up To Handle The Special Needs Horse? ...205

Chapter 38 209

When a Horse Doesn't Fit the Program That You Offer......... 209

Chapter 39 213

You Can't Always Perceive How Your Clients Are Going To See Things 213

Chapter 40 216

Is Your Chore Routine Stressing Out the Horses In Your Care? 216

Chapter 41.. 220

Blanketing and How It Affects Your Job............................... 220

Chapter 42 229

Herd Management..229

Chapter 43 235

Mixed Herds or Not?..235

Chapter 44 238

No Two Horses Are the Same.. 238

Chapter 45 242

What Kind Of Clients and Horses Are You Trying To Attract? 242

Chapter 46 247

You're Clientele Will Change as Your Business Grows. Are You Ready? 247

Chapter 47 252

What Is So Important About a Clean Barn Anyway?...............252

Chapter 48 255

Boundaries 255

Chapter 49 261

Extra Charges for Services Done 261

Chapter 50 269

The Difference Between the Barn Owner and Barn Manager 269

Chapter 51 277

Educating Will Be Part of the Job 277

Chapter 52 280

The Financials 280

Chapter 53 285

Are You Willing to Ask a Boarder to Leave For the Betterment of Your Barn? 285

Chapter 54 289

Habits of Highly Successful Horse Professionals 289

Chapter 55 299

Don't Be Intimidated By What Other Boarding Facilities Say They Offer 299

Chapter 56 304

During Sickness and in Health 304

Chapter 57 308

Okay, So You Made a Poor Decision 308

Chapter 58 311

Creating a Team at Your Barn 311

Chapter 59 313

Take the High Road-Even When it is Difficult to Do 313

Chapter 60 315

Can You Make a Living At Boarding Horses? 315

Chapter 61 318
Don't Give Up, the Days Will Get Easier 318

Are you ready to make positive changes to your horse business? If you are, then I encourage you to keep reading and learn how your barn and horse business can change for the better. Through small changes you make one day at a time will emerge the business person and leader you always knew you could be, and it will change your barn, business and life for the better.

The Reason I Wrote This Book

The reason I wrote this book was because I found out very early on in our horse boarding business that I was going to need to make many changes and I had no idea where to start. What looks good on paper is many times different when you are in the thick of it every day. I couldn't find any books that talked about the issues I was having as a barn owner/manager and my first couple of years were tough ones.

Many people have the knowledge to take care of the horses at their barn but they quickly learn that they need some help and guidance when it comes to their clients. Changes in the first few years of business is very common for most new barn owners or barn managers and learning to become a leader and make those changes with confidence takes time. If you are ready to streamline and simplify your horse business and learn to make decisions and changes with confidence then I encourage you to keep reading. I truly believe that if you keep going even on those tough days and make changes when you need to, you will see your horse business grow and become strong and healthy.

I wrote this book to give encouragement and guidance to others that are struggling with some of the issues I struggled with early on in our horse business.

About This Book

Are you ready to make the positive changes in your barn and business but didn't know where to start or how to do it? If that is the case, you are not alone. Learning to deal with horses and people together takes time. When we were starting our boarding business, I couldn't find one book that dealt with horse barn management and the owner/client relationship.

Whether you are running your own horse barn or are just starting out in your equine business venture this book will change how you look at your barn, your business and even your life.

It may sound bold to say this book will change your life, but if you are running a horse business and are having a difficult time with your clients it will eventually migrate into other areas. If your relationship with your clients is strained then it will affect your personal life and that is the solid truth.

I learned this first hand when we built our barn and opened our business. I understood a lot about horses but had poor business skills and I didn't have a clue how to deal with my boarders in many situations. It took me years to figure out that good barn management has just as much to do with people as it has to do with horse care!

A good barn manager knows his horses and what they need to keep them safe, healthy and content. He knows when one of them is not feeling well or is lame. A barn manager knows how to keep a barn organized and efficient. The basic chores of feeding, cleaning stalls and turnout are all part of the job.

The bigger question would be what makes a *great* barn manager? What about when the day doesn't go as planned? What about when a horse gets hurt and the owner wants to put the blame on another horse and feelings get hurt in the process. How do you handle the upset boarder? I realized very early on in my career that I was leaving out a huge part of the equation for running a horse business. I was leaving out the people part.

Dealing with clients, both equine and human is equally important and learning to handle each situation takes time. In this book I share the mistakes I made through the years and what changes I made to make things much better at our barn. Many of the changes I needed to make were within me and how I was leading the barn and business.

Many people get into the horse business because they love horses and believe it would be the perfect career. I was that same person years ago. I love horses and there is nothing better than walking out to the barn each morning and hearing nickers as I come through the doors. Ten years ago I started a horse boarding business along with my husband David and we never looked back. There was just one problem. I was not a business person. I started a business with absolutely no business skills! I was running a horse business like a hobby farm and that does not work if you want to be successful.

Over the last couple of years I have had the pleasure of talking with so many barn owners that share their stories with me and many of them are going through the same struggles I did. Making the transition from someone that loves horses to someone that is running a horse business and still loves horses can take time with growing pains along the way. This book is about becoming the business person you need to be to handle every situation that will come your way. It is about learning to deal with an upset client in a positive and professional way and learning to have confidence in all your decisions. This book is about learning to run your barn with confidence.

I truly believe once you learn to become a confident leader and barn owner, your business will take off in ways you never imagined. Your boarders want to know that the person who is taking care of their horse knows what they are doing and when clients leave the barn, they need to know that their horse is safe and in competent, caring hands.

Your horse business will go through many changes especially in the first few years and that is always difficult for a new start-up business. You are also going to change from within as you become the business person you need to be to run a healthy horse business. If you are ready to make your horse business all that it can be then I encourage you to keep reading and be open to a barn management makeover. It will change your barn, business and your life for the better.

Take a chance, make some needed changes and positive things will happen.

Chapter 1

Open for Business. Are You Ready?

No matter what part of the horse industry you are in, the opening day of your business will be the most memorable. You only get one grand opening and we all want it to be the very best day possible.

I can remember our grand opening day like it was yesterday. It was July and the weather was gorgeous. We were expecting the first two of thirty something horses to arrive at our farm and I was completely over the moon with excitement. Inside I was wishing that all the horses would come on the same day but I am sure glad they didn't. I was in for the shock of my life.

The first horses came and I will never forget those first hours after the trailers pulled in. One of the horses was an Arabian and the other was a tall Appendix Quarter Horse. They were the only two that came that first day but getting them situated and making sure their owners were comfortable with the place was an all-day affair.

By the time we hit early August our barn and outdoor board were completely full and I was running on less sleep than I ever imagined. I had become a business woman and barn manager overnight and I was not prepared for all that came with it. I had done everything to prepare myself up to that point but it was nothing compared to actually living it every day.

I found myself spending many long hours in the barn answering questions frequently and changing things from stall assignments to grain and supplements. And that was just the beginning.

Not ready for opening day

Over the last year, I have talked with many barn owners that have walked that same path as I did and they have all said the same thing. They truly were not ready for opening day and all the work that came with it.

There are so many things to think about when you are running a horse facility. When you have thirty something horses come to your farm and you have no prior experience with any of those horses and their personalities, it becomes a new level of barn management. Where do you begin? Do you just start putting horses together and hope they get along? Those were things that I had not thought out real well and I must admit it was a guessing game the first few months.

Things are so much different now. Horses don't leave our barn very often but when a new horse does come to live at our farm, I already know the personalities of each herd and every horse that is on our property. This makes it so much easier when I am deciding where to place a new horse.

If you are opening a new horse business, you are going to spend many hours adjusting things that need changing after you are in operation. What looks like a good idea sometimes isn't and you need to be ready and be flexible to change things for the betterment of your barn.

You will make more changes in your barn and how it is run during the first three to four years than you will the rest of your career. How you run your business regarding the owner/client relationship will change also and grow as time goes on. How you handle your paperwork and rules will change during that time. Your fees will change a few times during those early years because I truly believe you cannot get an accurate account of the cost to run a horse farm until you have gone through all four seasons a couple of times. It took us about three years to figure out the true cost of everything from hay and grain to electricity and gasoline to run the equipment. You also have to account for damage done by horses. Even if the owner of the horse will pay for the damage, there is still time and labor. It is all part of the equation.

It's a business first

People will ask me what they can do to better prepare for owning their own business in the horse world. I always tell them to first take some business classes so they understand the business side of it. The most important thing to remember is that it is a business first. Many farms go under because the owners are not running it like a business.

The second thing I recommend is to work on an established horse farm for a while and ask the owner's if you can see how the entire operation works from sun up to sun down. Remember this will be a seven-day a week job and the days are long and the job still needs to get done no matter what the weather is. Get your boots muddy and dive in and learn as much as you can. It will make your transition to business owner that much easier.

You will still have opening day shock the first few weeks but I can assure you that it will be a time to celebrate and the transition to business owner will be much easier if you really take time to prepare for it.

Chapter 2

What Barn Management is to Most People

My idea of what horse barn management is has changed so much over the years. I am no different than most people who have the dream of owning and running their own horse boarding business. I got into it because I love horses and my husband loves working on the farm. We believed we had a good foundation of what horse care is all about. Most of us start out the same way thinking it will be a pretty nice career. At least that is how I was feeling years ago before we built our barn and opened Vinland Stables.

Barn management to most people is pretty straight forward. Your job responsibilities will differ a little depending on what kind of horse barn you establish or work at. If you are boarding a small number of horses and most of them live outside all year round your job will be much less involved but the core care will always stay the same.

You might not have a huge number of stalls to clean every day but checking out each horse to make sure they are healthy and free of cuts and abrasions is something that all barn owners and barn managers should be doing on a daily basis. Making sure they are maintaining their ideal weight and not stressed in the herd you have placed them in is important and something that should be checked regularly.

If you are running a large facility with many horses, then your job responsibilities are going to be more detailed. Your barn could be a breeding barn with many babies or it could be a show barn with jumpers. Your barn might be a multi-discipline barn where you could have a huge variety of breeds and with the different breeds comes some different needs. Each of these types of barns will come with their own set of responsibilities for the care of the horses living there. It is all part of horse barn management.

If you go to college for equine management, they will educate you on barn management and how to run a horse barn. A person who is knowledgeable in barn management should have a good foundation of horse care and horsemanship. They should have some knowledge of basic medical care and understand the nutritional needs of each horse in their care. They need to know herd management and have a good understanding of horse behavior. In many barns the barn manager will clean stalls, feed horses, turn horses out each morning and bring them in each afternoon.

Okay, so what is the problem?

Okay, so you are wondering what the problem is? It seems so easy and straight forward. That is exactly what I thought also. I was ready to take care of forty horses at our farm when we opened. The part of the puzzle that is missing and is vital to running a healthy horse facility is the people part.

As a barn manager you are going to have clients from all walks of life. Some of your clients will be very easy to work with and some of them are going to make you want to quit your job. The horse part will be the easiest part of your day.

Becoming a great barn manager takes skill and knowledge in horse care but it also takes skill in people care. Behind every successful horse barn is a person running it that has great interpersonal skills. They are very professional and very good at dealing with clients and co-workers. They can see the storm clouds brewing ahead of time and know how to settle everyone down when drama hits the barn. They know how to lead with confidence and understand not everyone will agree with their decisions but they are doing it for the betterment of the barn and horses. A great barn manager looks at each client and horse and meets them where they are with their skill and knowledge level and helps them grow. They know how to create strong relationships with their clients and are not afraid to address concerns even when they know they will be tough ones to deal with.

The bottom line

The bottom line is you are going to be dealing with people on an everyday basis. When the weather is great and the sun is out people are always in a good mood and easy to be around. They can ride outside and enjoy the day and it will feel like you have the best job in the world.

The day will come when the weather has been cold and wet for it seems weeks and everyone is in a bad mood and all of a sudden nothing is good enough anymore. Sometimes your boarders will start looking and comparing your barn to other places and what they offer. They might wonder why other barns already have their horses turned out on grass and your barn has not done that yet. They will wonder why your place is so muddy compared to other boarding places. These are very real issues that all barn owners and managers deal with.

If you are in the business long enough, you will eventually have a horse or two that cannot keep out of trouble. You will have a horse that always seems to be getting hurt or is always lame for one reason or another. How are you going to handle those issues especially when the owner of the horse wants to blame another horse? You may end up with problems and hurt feelings between the owners of both horses. If you think this won't happen, let me be the first to tell you that it will. What happens to the horse extends to the owner and they will want answers. Are you ready to reassure them and stand your ground? What if your reassurance isn't enough and they want change?

Don't forget about the people

Complete horse barn management is about horse care and people care. It is a great job and I love my job now but when we opened our barn I didn't like my job at all for the first three years. I was in shock some days with what I saw happening in our barn and I had to learn from trial and error how to handle each situation that presented itself. I didn't have anyone to go to for advice and I couldn't find any books that addressed barn management and the client.

This book is going to address many parts of horse barn management like you have never heard before. You will realize you are not alone in your business venture. Having good horse knowledge is a must if you are going to run a horse barn, but you must have good leadership skills if you want to keep your barn running smoothly and efficiently. It doesn't happen overnight and for me it took about five years before I was comfortable in my skin as a barn owner and manager. It was through all the mistakes I made early on that I grew as a confident barn owner.

If you are ready to fix the problems at your barn and make a positive difference then I encourage you to keep reading. Remember, sometimes we learn the most through adversity and trials that come our way and if we don't give up, they will make us stronger. That is true in life and business. Start one day at a time making the positive changes you want at your barn and watch your business grow. It will happen.

Chapter 3

Let's Start With the Easy Part-The Barn Chores

I love getting up early each morning (most days) and going out into the barn. The stillness of the early morning and the fact that the only sound I hear each morning are nickers when I turn on the lights never gets old. Doing the basic barn chores of feeding hay, grain and turning the horses out for the day is the easy part of my job. It is physical and once in a while I have a horse that is not very patient but for the most part, it goes pretty smoothly. David and I have a system down that works like clockwork and we each know our jobs. I take care of all the grain, supplements and medicines and he is busy feeding hay outside during that time. Once he is done feeding, we start walking the horses outside.

Every barn is going to run a little differently and how you do your barn chores will depend on if your horses go outside for the day or stay inside. It will depend on the weather and if you have shelters in your paddocks or not. People are always amazed at how fast we can feed, grain and turnout all the horses each morning. We usually start around five in the morning with chores and by seven o'clock they are all outside until it's time to bring them back in.

Just like any other job

The one thing that David and I do is that we treat our barn chores just like any other job that most people have. Now we don't really clock in but you could set your clock by when our barn lights go on each morning. It is great for us to keep everything consistent and it is extremely good for the horses. They know what to expect and if you have been around horses then you already know how impatient they can be when they have to wait a long time.

Another reason that we like to start our chores at the same time each day is because then I can make other plans during the day if I need to and it is never a guessing game. One of the biggest compliments I get from our boarders every now and then is how consistent we are. They don't have to worry that their horse has not been fed when they come out to the barn early in the morning. They know if they are going to a horse show or trail ride that things are going to be done and it makes the boarder feel so much better and confident about the care that is given to their horse.

I know at our barn we start very early in the morning but it works for us. I am a morning person and I don't mind getting up and my husband likes to get out of the barn before the boarders start to arrive. It doesn't mean you have to do your chores this way but a consistent chore schedule is a win/win for both the horses and their owners.

May I give one bit of advice-whatever time you decide to start your chores at your farm, be consistent. It can be very stressful on a horse when one morning they are fed at five and the next morning they are fed at nine. It happens all the time on farms and horses do much better if they know what to expect. Some horses might not get so upset but many of them will show anxiety in many different ways including kicking their stalls and weaving. Many vices start to show their ugly head when a horse becomes stressed.

It takes so much longer than I thought

Another problem I hear about when it comes to barn chores is how long everything takes to do. Many people become very surprised when they start taking care of a large number of horses on their farm. What used to only take an hour to do with a few horses now takes several hours and it can burn a person out very fast if they don't know how to stream line their barn chores.

We have forty horses and I have streamlined it so that we can get everything done in an amount of time that is very reasonable. Are we hustling? Yes we are, but we know what our job is and we do it. Organization is a key part to barn chores. So many barns are set up in a way that makes feeding and doing grain and supplements very time consuming. What should only take an hour can end up taking several hours on a large farm if they are poorly organized.

If you feel like your barn chores are taking too long then look at your set up and find ways to streamline it. I would encourage you to look at how other barns do their chores and ask for advice. You can ask ten different barn owners how they do their chores and they will most likely all be a little different but that is good. It will give you a very clear view of how to do things and you can pick and choose what works for you and give it a try. You can always change it if it's not working.

Chapter 4

Stall Cleaning and Bedding

When we opened our barn with twenty-seven stalls I knew I was going to be doing a lot of stall cleaning. I was ready for it and I have always enjoyed mucking out stalls. In many ways I find it therapeutic and when I talk with other horse crazy people they say the same thing. I would rather clean stalls than my house!

The one thing I was not prepared for were some of the different opinions on how stalls should be cleaned and bedded. I have worked at a few barns in my life and some of them bed very heavy and some bed light. Depending on how a stall is bedded will make a huge difference in how long it takes to clean it. Because our horses go outside almost every day we decided to bed the stalls on the lighter side. There is no right or wrong way to do this. It is just a personal preference.

Our stalls have rubber mats with shavings over them so cleaning is easy. We clean and then sweep the shavings half way back and then add fresh. It works well and we rarely have a urine smell.

Double checking my work

Over the years I have had boarders come from other barns that wanted their shavings piled up in the middle. I have had boarders come from other barns where the stalls were not cleaned on a regular basis (even though they paid for it). They would come out every day to check their stall to make sure it was cleaned to their satisfaction. I actually had one lady walk through her stall and move the shavings around with her boot to make sure it was clean and if it wasn't clean enough she would let me know. Talk about pressure.

I have learned now that the reason many boarders might seem difficult when it comes to stall cleaning is only because they have experienced a bad boarding situation where their stall didn't get cleaned as promised. Bad boarding experiences will always carry over to the next place until they feel confident that their horse is going to be taken care of and that even includes stall cleaning.

Opinions about shavings

There are also many opinions about shavings and what kind to use. I have seen it all. When we first opened we tried bagged shavings. They were a beautiful quick pick type of shavings that smelled great. We bought a huge number of bags to start off with when we first opened and I soon realized how much work bagged shavings were. Not only did we have to open twenty-seven bags almost every day but I had to get them to each stall which was a lot of work. I was making several trips in a large wheelbarrow down our long barn aisle and I think putting the shavings in the stalls was much harder work than actually cleaning them!

You don't realize how much work something is until you have to do it twenty-seven times! Everything is easy when you only have one or two horses but if you are running a larger barn then this will be something you are going to want to think about.

After we were done with all those bags of shavings we switched to bulk shavings and it has worked out so much better and has saved me a ton of money over the years. Some people might argue that you never know what you are going to get with bulk shavings, but I disagree.

Get to know your shavings supplier

If you have a good working relationship with the person you buy your bulk shavings from and he knows what you want for the stalls, then you will find that most of the time your shavings will be great. There has only been one time in the last ten years that we received extremely dusty shavings and I called our shavings supplier and he brought us a different load. Remember, you need to communicate and don't settle for less but be professional when you are discussing any problems that come up.

I had a boarder once that didn't like our shavings because she thought they were too fine. She liked the big fluffy kind and I would try to share with her that the big flaked shavings don't absorb the urine as well as the finer shavings. She didn't get it. She wanted that fresh look that you see when you go to the county fair and walk in the barns to look at the animals. The stalls all look beautiful and pristine.

What she didn't realize is that those stalls are cleaned probably three or four times a day with shavings added quite often. If you can afford to offer that service at your barn that is great, but in the real world of horses and business it is not practical. If you are going to offer a service like that, it will need to reflect in your board price because your shavings cost will go through the roof. Shavings will be your second highest cost next to hay and most people don't realize that when they set their board rate.

You will always have one person that might not like how you do things at your barn with your bedding and shavings. You need to do what is best for your barn and what you use for bedding is your final decision. If someone leaves because they didn't like the bedding then I don't believe the problem was with only the bedding to begin with. You might need to look deeper into the situation and find out if there were other things that were bothering this person and the bedding was just a trigger.

Your boarders will always have different opinions regarding horse care and they have that right. As the barn owner you need to look at the big picture and do what is right for your business even if there is someone that doesn't agree.

Remember that if they like your barn and the care is good, most of the time people will stop trying to find something to complain about and start to trust you. They start to realize that their horse is in great hands at your barn and they are happy and healthy. That is the bottom line. Once your clients start to trust you things will only get better from there.

Chapter 5

Hay, Grain and Supplements

When it comes to hay, grain and supplements there is a lot you could talk about. There are many books out there on feeding horses and what is best. In this book I am not going to talk about how much hay to feed or what kinds of grain to use. I am not going to give you my opinion on what supplements work well and which ones don't.

This book is not about nutrition and the horse. This book is about how to make your job easier and more efficient and how to deal with your clients when it comes to hay, grain and supplements. I hope I have your attention because there is a lot to talk about.

Feeding Hay

When we first opened our boarding business I was not prepared for all the opinions on hay. I had boarded my own horses for many years growing up in California and I don't ever once remember questioning the barn owner about the type of hay that was being fed. At many of the boarding barns the horses seemed well fed. I did experience one place that didn't feed enough hay to my horse and she lost a lot of weight but I was young and had a lot to learn back then about hay and how much to feed.

Before we had built our barn I had four horses that I took care of here on our farm and the hay we were feeding was great. It was a grass mix and our horses did really well on it. Once we built our barn and we were taking care of a large number of horses, we needed to buy hay in extremely large quantities. We had always used small bales that were about fifty pounds each but we decided to try the large bales that weigh about nine hundred pounds each.

The first load of large bales we purchased came from a guy I didn't know at all. I found his add in the paper and so I thought we would try him. He delivered a hundred large bales and guaranteed us that the hay would not be moldy. I was about to learn a big lesson.

I paid the man and he left. As we started opening the bales, one by one the hay inside was partly moldy. It became a disaster quickly. We were a brand new business with brand new boarders that didn't even know us and we had moldy hay! I tried to get hold of the guy many times over the next several weeks and he never returned my calls. I didn't know where he lived and because I was a brand new barn owner with no business experience, I didn't know what to do at the time but give up. David spent that entire winter tearing apart those bales and throwing out a ton of hay. We lost thousands of dollars and the stress was incredible.

Not only was our hay bad that first year but our boarders noticed how bad the hay was. Thank goodness we had a barn full of small bales that we could also feed otherwise I believe we would have lost many boarders that first year due to our poor quality hay.

The next summer we started buying from our neighbor who is a farmer. He makes the large bales and brings us great hay. I was happy with our hay and we were feeding a grass/alfalfa mix or mostly grass hay. I thought most of our boarders were happy with our hay but I was about to learn a new lesson about running a business and people. There are always going to be some people that are not happy with what you offer at your barn and you need to understand this and stand your ground on your choice of hay you feed. If you don't you will soon become very stressed trying to please everyone.

During the second year of our business I had a boarder that decided that our hay was not good enough and started bringing his own hay. He wanted to feed his horse pure alfalfa and he asked me if he could store it in the back hay room. He told me he wanted his horse to have some "good hay" every day. I was in shock to say the least. I was dealing with a new problem that I never imagined would be an issue.

I talked with my husband and told him the situation about this guy wanting to keep his hay in our hay room. My husband told him no and that he would need to keep his hay at home. What happened next became a bigger problem.

He would come each day with his own hay and carry it through the barn and the other boarders would see the hay and of course ask what he was feeding. Before long I had others asking about the hay. It started to become a problem and I was becoming nervous that others would start to feel our hay was not good enough. We were a new business and we were still trying to earn a good reputation and it is very hard when you have clients bringing in their own hay because yours is not "good enough" in their mind.

After several months of this we finally had a discussion with these people and told them that we felt our hay was very good nutritionally for the horses. I even had our hay tested to make sure I knew what I was talking about. The situation settled down for everyone except this one boarder that eventually left and that was okay. The barn atmosphere changed for the better and it was a great learning experience for me.

If you are going to run a boarding barn then be prepared because you will come across many different people with different views about feeding hay. You need to be prepared for the unexpected like someone bringing in their own hay because they feel yours is not good enough. Part of barn management is learning to deal with clients under all circumstances even the stressful ones.

I encourage you to have a game plan for this kind of situation because if you board horses long enough you will come across the boarder who wants to bring their own hay. If you want to allow them to bring hay that is perfectly fine but you need to look at the big picture. One boarder bringing their own hay is no big deal but if you have ten boarders bringing their own hay and they all want to store it in the hay room, it will become a huge headache for you.

If your barn starts to get the reputation that the boarders bring their own hay because they don't like the hay you feed, that will NOT be good for your business! Potential new boarders will wonder why people bring their own hay and there is a good chance it will frighten them off.

Remember, most of your boarders will have very little knowledge about hay and the different types of hay. They are depending on you to educate them if they have questions. If you don't help them understand then they will follow what they see others doing and that includes bringing their own hay. As the barn owner you will have to lead and a big part of your job will be educating your clients.

The bottom line is that your boarders just want to make sure their horse is getting fed enough good quality hay. It is your job to help them find that place where they feel good about the feed and care. If you take the time to educate and reassure them it will pay off in the long run and you will have clients that trust you and stay for a long time.

Buying hay will be the biggest expense you have on your farm. If you are able to make some of your own hay it will cut way down on the expense but most people don't have that kind of acreage. We make about a quarter of all our hay and the rest we purchase. If you are going to purchase hay I strongly encourage you to know the person you are buying hay from and make sure they understand that the hay is for horses-NOT for cattle or goats! Also have some kind of return policy in writing if the hay is moldy or poor quality.

A farmer can do his very best to grow good quality hay but once in a while mother nature will not cooperate and he might have a hard time drying the hay. We will find a bad bale once in a great while and we have an arrangement with the farmer to exchange the bad bale for a good bale of hay. He feeds the hay that is not good for horses to his cattle and he gives us a new bale that is for horses. We have done this for years and it is a great working arrangement. I know not everyone can have this kind of arrangement but it is vital to talk with your hay supplier and find out what arrangement can be made if you buy hay that you can't feed to your horses. Don't buy until you are completely happy with the business agreement regarding the hay you are buying.

You have too much on the line financially and with your business reputation. It is not worth the risk of losing thousands of dollars or losing clients because you don't want to offend the seller.

If you are buying from someone you don't know I recommend getting some references and ask what his return policy is on moldy hay. Get a written receipt with a guarantee of return on bad hay. You have too much on the line financially and with your business reputation. It is not worth the risk of losing thousands of dollars or clients because you don't want to offend the seller.

Remember that you are running a business and you need to be smart about it now. I wish someone would have shared this with us when we bought our first hundred large bales of hay. It would have saved us thousands of dollars and lots of worry and stress that first year.

Feeding Grain

Feeding grain to horses can either be very easy or you can make it hard and complicated. Most boarding barns that offer grain will feed it two times a day. If you only have a handful of horses to feed, usually it is a simple thing. If you have a lot of horses like we do at our barn, it can be very complicated if you allow it to be.

When we first opened years ago we included grain as part of the board. We provided a general maintenance grain and allowed up to four pounds a day per horse. Many people used our grain and then we had some boarders that chose to supply their own. It worked out great at first but a few years ago the grain prices started to increase dramatically and we were losing a lot of money each month. I knew it was time to change things at our barn but it was not going to be popular with our boarders.

Every barn in our area included grain as part of the monthly board and we were about to change that. We decided that we would supply three types of grain to make it easier for our clients but they would need to pay the cost of what their horse was eating each month.

I offered a general purpose grain, a high performance grain and a senior grain and I would only charge what my cost was. Because I was buying in large quantities I knew I could save them a little money. If a boarder wanted to supply their own grain, they still could.

When I let our client's know about the change, I gave them two months to decide what they wanted to do. I was very worried that we were going to lose many boarders over this because our board was already on the upper end for our area and every other barn included grain as part of the board.

What I had to do next was extremely important. I needed to educate my boarders on marketing and explain to them that the other barns are not offering grain for "Free." Their board prices were higher than ours for a comparable facility and that was partly to cover the cost of the grain. They were just packaging what they offered differently. You need to remember that no one goes into business to lose money and nothing is free. The cost will come from somewhere and the client needs to understand this.

You need to remember that no one goes into business to lose money and nothing is free. The cost will come from somewhere and the client needs to understand this.

I like to use the example of shopping to buy a new automobile. When you talk with the dealer they will work very hard to make a sale and many times they will throw in extras and tell you "At no extra charge." The reality is that someone is paying for those "Extras." Car dealers are there to make money and lots of it. They can't make money if they give away free extras all the time.

It all comes around and you might get a few extras free but they know what their margin of profit is and they are very sure they are not going to go below it. This is true for any business that wants to make a profit and not lose money. Your horse business will be exactly the same.

After much talk and a little educating and reassurance we changed how we did things regarding grain and we only lost one boarder over this issue. I must say I have never regretted that decision and now I know exactly how much money is going out monthly on grain and I am not losing a penny.

Keep things simple

I have talked with barn owners that became frustrated because they were trying to offer too many different types of grain for their boarders and they changed grains all the time. What makes it more complicated is that each brand of grain is a different price. Prices in grain will vary from brand to brand and it will get complicated very quickly. It will make your book keeping more difficult and confusing so I encourage you to keep it as simple as you can.

If I can give some advice, only offer a few types of grain for your boarders. If they want something different then let them be responsible for going to the feed store and bringing it back to the barn. We have had a few boarders over the years that changed their grain type often but because they were buying their own grain, it was completely up to them to do the changing in the grain bin. If they wanted to do the work that was fine with me.

You will always have a client here or there that will change things quite frequently and as the barn manager you need to decide where your job responsibility starts and ends with the grain.

Remember, you will burn out fast if you are spending hours each month dealing with grain changes and figuring out prices, adjustments and cost. You are not running a feed store so keep it simple.

Giving Supplements

Over the last ten years I have seen so many different kinds of supplements come through our barn and all of them promise grand results. There are complete magazines on supplements for horses and they can come in pellet, paste, powder or oil.

If you are offering to feed supplements then you will want to think through the easiest way to feed them every day. Remember if you only have a few horses then it is no big deal but if you are taking care of many horses then you are going to want to make your job efficient.

I must admit, I was only used to feeding my four horses supplements but after we built our barn and I had to feed forty horses supplements with their grain, it became overwhelming at times. I had looked at how other barns did this part of chore time but every barn did it differently and some seemed very complicated and very confusing.

Right from the start I decided that if a boarder had more than one type of supplement for their horse they would need to put the supplements in a baggie or small container for each feeding. This has worked out great because I have horses that only get one supplement but I have many that get two or three supplements a day.

I didn't want to have sixty different supplement containers to open up on a daily basis. Requiring baggies or containers for multi-supplements has made my job so much easier. The other part of the equation is space. Where are you going to store all these containers of supplements and have easy access to them once or possibly twice a day?

Everything you do at your barn will be motivated by time and time is money. They are all strongly connected.

One more very important part of the equation is the type of supplements. Pellets are always the easiest but many supplements will come in a powder form and you will have client's that will want you to feed a powder. Powders are great as long as the horse eats it.

Some horses become very smart and leave the powder at the bottom of the corner feeder. You might get a request to add water to the grain/supplement mix if the horse doesn't eat the powder. I never mix the water in the grain bucket because it makes a real wet mess of the bucket and the powder sticks to the sides of the bucket and can become moldy. I have also had the problem of the buckets sticking together due to all the powder that is stuck to the sides of the bucket. It is best to keep water or any type of liquid out of your grain buckets.

There are many supplements that come in an oil form. Let me be the first to say it is a real mess! Feeding oils of any kind whether it is for joint lubrication or to put weight on a horse is a pain.

There is no easy way to feed oils and if you add it to your grain bucket, you will have even more of a mess. Some joint supplements can be squeezed right out of the bottle and into the corner feeder and that works but many of them don't come that way.

We also had another issue with the oils. Our barn is not heated and in Wisconsin the winters can get pretty cold and everything freezes including your oils. We tried giving oils in the early years of our business and after a while I decided enough was enough. I had a sticky mess in the summer and thick almost frozen oil in the winter that was hard to get out of the bottle. I decided it was time to simplify this part of our program.

I sent out a letter explaining that we would no longer be giving any supplements that came in an oil form and also tried to educate our boarders and explain that there were plenty of products out there that would do the same thing without the mess. We stopped using oils at our farm and it has made the job so much easier.

If you only have a few horses to take care of then these little things like oil supplements might not seem like a big deal but if you are running a large horse facility, it will become a big deal very fast. If your barn is set up to handle all forms of supplements and you don't mind giving them then go for it. You will find what works best for your barn through many trials.

Remember that it is okay to tell your clients that you don't offer that particular service at your barn. I don't believe you will lose a boarder over something so little. We live in a time where there are so many great choices of supplements for the health of a horse and it is so much easier for a person to switch to something else if they need to.

Chapter 6

Open Seven Days a Week

I never realized what it really meant to be open seven days a week until we started our business. Many stores and businesses are open seven days a week and for the customer it is great. If we forget something at the market we can run there even if it is on Sunday. If we want to go shopping for new clothes we can go on Sunday. It is a wonderful convenience for the customer and we never give it any more thought until the day we become the business owner.

Once you become the owner of a business the responsibility becomes great and you really never stop thinking about it. If you are running a clothing store you might take off on a Sunday but you still have employees who will work. If one of them doesn't show up or calls in sick, you will be the one getting the call. If you don't have a back-up there is a good chance you will be working. It just comes with business ownership.

The world of horses and horse business is no different and because horses need to be fed and watered at least twice a day, seven days a week, the job will not end on Saturday evening or holidays. Another part of the picture is your clients. Our barn is open for our boarders to come see their horse 365 days a year. We have people at our barn every day of the year and holidays are no exception.

Seven days a week

When we first opened our barn I not only had to get used to caring for many horses seven days a week but I also had to get used to having people at our farm seven days a week. This was something I had not given any thought to before we built our barn and I must be very honest and tell you it was a huge adjustment. Not only was I exhausted all the time from the work but now I felt the pressure of being personable with the boarders even on the weekends when I really didn't want to see or talk with people.

Owning and running a business that is not on your homestead property is one thing because you can go home at the end of the day and not see any customers. It is much different when your barn and business are just a few hundred feet from your house and people are coming in to see their horses all day long.

Over the years I have become used to the lifestyle of having a business on our property and I now can separate myself from my clients even if I need to work on the weekend. This is something I was not able to do in the beginning and it took me years to learn.

Your family will need some space

Our boarders now understand that my family needs our privacy and they really respect that and I appreciate it so much. It's not that I don't want to talk with anyone if it falls on a Sunday but if I am quiet while I am doing barn chores, I don't feel guilty for not talking and I don't put the added pressure on myself to always be "On" for them.

If you are new to running your barn and business I encourage you to try to find time each week to have some time off. If you are in a position to hire employees and have a day off from the barn then do it. Most young businesses are not in a position to hire employees. If you are doing the chores yourself every day then you need to come to a place where you realize it is okay to be quiet and just do your job.

It can wait until Monday

If your boarders want to ask you to do something that is not an emergency and it can wait until Monday then explain to them that you will get to it early Monday because you have other plans after you get the chores done. In most cases they will understand and you will start to feel the weight of your business lighten up a little.

I love being in the barn but even I can get burned out from it now and then. Trying to find a day off to get away even if it means relaxing in your home with a good book is extremely healthy for you, your family and your business.

I talk with many barn owners and many of them are burned out to the point where they want to sell their farm and quit the business. They haven't learned how to pace themselves and find a balance between work and rest. In a business where you are dealing with animals, your job really never ends but you can adjust it so that you have time to rest and rejuvenate yourself.

Make this area a priority in your life. It will not only benefit you but also your family and those around you. It will even benefit your clients indirectly because when you have time to rest and rejuvenate yourself, they will see the difference.

Chapter 7

Horses and Weather and the Many Different Opinions

Let me tell you right now that the four seasons you love and enjoy will greatly affect your job on the farm. I never gave the weather much thought being born and raised in Los Angeles, California but living here in Wisconsin is a completely different story. The weather in Wisconsin dictates everyday what we are doing with the horses. It changes so fast around here and we can start off with sixties one day and have snow the next. It is crazy to say the least.

The weather will play a big part on how you run your farm. If you live somewhere that has four complete seasons with extreme highs and lows in temperatures, it will definitely make your job more difficult at times.

Once you have your barn set up and you have gone through the seasons of weather at your horse farm, you will start to become familiar with what works best for the horses in your care. The more challenging part will be the people.

I had no idea there would be so many different opinions on weather and horses. In fact, I was very naïve when it came to dealing with people and their horses. I somehow just believed that the owners would have the same view I did about when the horses should go outside and when they should stay in. My life became very complicated our first winter (as a very new business owner) with the clients that boarded at our barn.

How we deal with the weather

At our farm we put the horses outside as much as possible. My husband is diligent about checking the weather every morning to see what the forecast is for the day. The horses that are stalled at night do not have shelters outside in the paddocks during the day so if the weather is calling for a lot of rain or sub-zero temperatures we leave the horses in. If the weather is cold but the air is calm with no wind then most days they will go outside. The wind chill can be a factor here in the Midwest.

If it is a warm summer day and we are going to get a light rain, the horses will go out but if a strong storm is coming in with lightning and thunder we bring them in. As you can see the list can go on and on and no two days are the same when it comes to the weather. It is something that every horse owner thinks about every day.

There were days when we had fresh snow on the ground and it was cold but the weather was pristine outside. I have had boarders that worried that their horses were too cold and would bring them in as soon as they got to the barn. They would even be upset at me for putting them outside in the first place.

To be honest I didn't get it at all. The weather was beautiful and they would rush out and bring their horses in and then their horses would call and pace the stalls because they were upset that the barn was empty and all the other horses were outside.

Horses love the snow and they will roll and run around and play and some clients will not understand this. I believe the owners can make the situation much worse because they are not educated on what signs to look for when a horse becomes cold or struggling in the weather.

Many times a person will be very cold (most likely because they are not dressed for the weather) and they just assume their horse is cold. They forget that a horse is built differently and even the thin skinned horses like thoroughbreds love being outside. They might need to be blanketed but they still would prefer to be outside.

You can't please everyone

We are pretty conservative at our barn and we don't put the horses outside if the weather is going to be bad and this also became a problem because we had boarders that wanted their horse outside no matter what the weather was. They didn't care if the weather was extremely cold with a below zero wind-chill or pouring down rain and a high of maybe fifty degrees.

These types of clients have what I call the "Wild horse out on the range" mentality. They believe that the horse was created to be outside and they are a hearty animal. What they fail to understand is that the horses in our care are not wild mustangs that know how to endure the weather out west. They are domesticated horses that are solely dependent on us for their survival. They get their food, water and shelter from us and they need us to keep them safe. There is a huge difference and some of your clients will not understand this.

The interesting thing about some people is that they will pay a lot for monthly stall board because they want their horse in a stall at night but want to treat them like a wild horse during the day. The two worlds do not mix very well and as the barn owner, you will need to figure out where you stand on the issue of weather and the horses in your care.

If you are going to board horses for a living then you need to be prepared for both types of boarders. There are the people that become upset because you put their horse outside and ones that become upset because you left them inside for the day. It will truly be a balancing act and there are going to be times when you need to make a decision on whether the horses go out or stay in and you need to stick by it and not worry about.

At the end of the day, you need to do what is best for the barn and the horses in your care and you can't always worry about an upset boarder. If you worry about every decision you make, you will drive yourself crazy and your business will start to become weak because of your indecisiveness.

When the weatherman gets it wrong

There have been many mornings when we have watched the weather and they called for extremely strong storms with high winds and it turned out to be a beautiful day. There have even been times when they have called for sunshine and clear skies and a huge storm comes up fast and we are scrambling to get all the horses back in their stalls. As the barn owner, you can only go by what the weather is predicting for the moment and your boarders need to understand this. Over the years I have had a few upset boarders because we have left the horses inside for the day and the weather turned out to be very nice later on.

At our barn once we make the call to leave all the horses in for the day, we do not put them outside later on if the weather clears up. If you have employees that can do this then that is great but most barns don't have employees scheduled all day to put horses outside or leave in depending on the weather.

If we have made the call to leave the horses inside for the day and the weather turns out to be nice later on, we do allow our boarders to come and put their horse outside if they would like. The only rule we have is that if you put your horse outside then you are responsible for bringing them back in. This system has worked great over the years for us and our boarders.

If the weather is good in the morning and they are not calling for rain until later on in the day, we will put the horses outside even if it is for only a few hours just to get them out to stretch their legs.

Flexibility and the size of your barn

With a large size barn and many horses, the flexibility of how it is run will be slightly different depending on the staff that is available. Each barn is going to do things differently and depending on the size of your facility and where you live will affect how you choose to do things on a daily basis with turnout and the weather.

Remember that not everyone will always agree with how you do things and you are going to have to find a way to earn the trust of your boarders. Once they know you put the horses first in all situations they will start to relax and the job will become much easier.

Part of the reason we were having so many problems early on in our business with clients and turnout, I believe was because they didn't know us and they didn't trust us. Many of them had come from places where the care was bad and they were not ready to trust David and me.

It takes time to figure out how you are going to do things in all types of weather and I really think you need to go through a couple of years of dealing with the four seasons to find out what works best at your farm and to become confident in your decisions. Once you get to that point, your boarders will see the confidence in you and it will make them feel much better.

The problems that happen between a barn owner and boarder often start because there is a lack of trust. It is a very scary thing to leave your horse at a place and wonder if they are going to be taken care of. Once you earn a reputation for great care in all types of weather, most of these problems will disappear.

Chapter 8

Not Enough Paddocks is a Problem

When I talk with other barn owners and hear about some of the issues they are having, one of the most common problems they talk about is how often the horses get hurt out in the herds. After a few minutes of listening to them I quickly realize that one of the reasons they are having more than their share of problems is because they have too many horses in too small of an area and not enough paddocks.

Putting horses together into small herds takes patience and a willingness to spend time observing the horses to make sure they are compatible. In most cases horses will figure it out and get along but what if they don't? What if you only have a couple of options for moving a horse that is getting beat up and he doesn't do well in either of those options? The reality is that some horses are not going to get along. It doesn't matter how small or large your paddocks are, if you are boarding horses there is going to come a time when you will have a horse that just doesn't fit in well with other horses.

Over the last ten years there have been several times when I have had to move a new horse a few times to find a herd that was a better fit. The reasons can be many and we may not ever know why some horses don't fit in well in certain herds but I am glad that we have many paddocks to work with.

Many farms operate under the view of all mares in one herd and all geldings in another. They might put twenty horses together and if they have the land and space for the horses to get away from each other than that is fine. Most people don't have that kind of acreage so with smaller paddocks the chances of a horse getting hurt becomes higher in a herd that is not accepting of him.

The farm with no option

Many potential boarders that come to my farm for a tour often tell me that the reason they want to move their horse is because their horse is getting beat up at their current stable. The farm has no option for them and if they don't do something fast they fear they are going to end up with a huge vet bill. I understand that completely. There is nothing more upsetting than to come out to see your horse and he is beat up day after day and it never ends.

Now I know that a horse can get hurt even in a very small herd and realistically you can have only two horses together in a paddock and you can still end up with a horse that is hurt due to a kick or bite. It is part of the world of horses but I also believe that if we are going to put them into herds, we should try our hardest to find a herd that is a good fit. Does it take work? Of course it does but it is well worth it once you find the right herd for a horse that is having a difficult time.

Plenty of paddocks should be a priority

If you are going to board horses and your place is going to offer turnout during the day, I encourage you to make sure you have plenty of paddocks. If you are designing your farm make this a high priority and if it means spending a little more on fencing then spend the money and do it right the first time. It is much easier to put up fencing and make a few more paddocks than to change it once the horses are at your barn and using it on a daily basis.

If you are already running a horse farm and you see that there are not enough paddocks and the horses are constantly getting into it with each other then make it a priority and start changing your fencing. Yes, it will be a pain and a lot of work but in the long run it will be so much easier than dealing with hurt horses and very upset owners.

Looking at the big picture

Remember, you have to look at the big picture about your business. What happens on your farm with any horse always includes having a discussion with the owner and you will be resolving many issues that didn't need to be there in the first place if you had a little more flexibility in paddocks.

What happens on your farm with any horse always includes having a discussion with the owner of the horse and you will be resolving many issues that didn't need to be there in the first place if you had a little more flexibility in paddocks.

There has never been a day since we opened our boarding business that I regretted all the extra work it was for us to make several extra paddocks for private turnout and even the senior horses in our care. From all our regular herds of horses to the horses that are mending from an injury and the senior horses that need a quieter turnout, having more paddocks has not only helped our business but made our job so much easier in every situation.

If you feel like you're having more than your share of issues with horses and herds and you are not sure where to turn, take a look at your paddocks and herd size. There is a good chance you might need to add some more paddocks for flexibility. It will truly make a difference with your barn, the horses in your care and your business. I guarantee that adding more paddocks to your farm will be an asset to your business and make your job so much easier in the long run.

Chapter 9

What Is Included In Your Job Description as Barn Owner or Barn Manager?

David and I learned more about running a horse business in the first two years of business than the last ten years all put together. We have been boarding horses now for a long time and how I looked at running our barn back then is so much different than how I do now. A lot has changed with my job description and it really has nothing to do with the chores I do every day.

As the owner of the business and also the barn manager I really didn't give any thought to what my job would include when we first opened. It seemed pretty straight forward and simple to me. David and I would feed horses and clean stalls. I would grain each horse and give supplements and the occasional medication as part of my job. We would put the horses outside each morning and bring then in each afternoon. There would be water buckets to fill and of course the cleaning was never ending.

I knew I would have boarders with questions now and then (especially if they were brand new horse owners) but for the most part I thought my life would be pretty simple and the boarders really wouldn't need much from me. Did I have a lot to learn about running a business!

It will consume you if you allow it

David and I didn't have a clear view of what our job descriptions were and before we knew it we were in the barn all the time and for much longer then we should have been. It started to consume us.

We were asked to do things that had nothing to do with what we offered here at our facility and we had not learned to say "no" at the time. Things got out of hand pretty quickly and I would receive calls as late as eleven at night about non-emergency issues and even early on Sunday mornings about non-emergency situations. With so many horses and people at our farm everything was magnified and I had to set some guidelines.

A perfect example of how your barn and job can consume you if you allow it is when the veterinarian comes out for a horse that needs medical attention. At our facility the vet comes out at least once a week for many different reasons. As the barn manager, do you feel you need to be there for every vet visit? That is a question you will need to ask yourself.

You will have boarders that will want support and ask you to be there. For me, I had to really decide if I needed to be there for each visit. Each situation will be different and even now I look at each vet visit on an individual basis. Most of the time I am not out there at all and then I will find out from the boarder what the veterinarian said. Occasionally there will be times that I know I need to be out there and it doesn't matter what time it is. I am good with that because I know the appointment is a serious one.

Most people that want to have a career with horses already have a good idea that it is not a nine to five job with weekends off. David and I knew that also. We were prepared to work seven days a week doing daily chores if we needed to and looking back that was the easy part. It was all the requests and needs of our clients early on that caught us off guard and we didn't know where to draw the line or how to say no to certain requests. It is very hard sometimes to find that line when you live on the same property as the business and you are open seven days a week. Your clients will forget at times that you really don't get a day off unless you leave town for a long weekend.

We have wonderful boarders at our barn and they know me pretty well and understand that my family needs our "time off" from working even if we are at home on the farm. This was something we didn't have in our early years and it is something that you need to establish. Make it clear to them and most of the time they will understand. If they don't understand then your barn might not be the right barn for them.

If you are going to run a horse business, then I encourage you to set guidelines and define what your job description is. There are going to be the times when an emergency happens and you need to be there but there will be many times when you don't need to be there and it will be fine. Setting boundaries and knowing what your job description really entails is so important for you and your family and your clients.

One last thought-If you are starting to feel stressed and mentally exhausted and spread too thin, there is a good chance you have not set up healthy boundaries and a clear job description in your horse business. Finding a balance is vital to lasting and not burning yourself out. Take time to talk with others in the same career as you and then find out what works best for your career and your family and stick to it. It will change your barn, business and life for the better.

Chapter 10

The Many Hats You Will Wear as the Barn Owner

Learning to run a large boarding facility came in many different dimensions. I was learning more than I ever dreamed about keeping a large facility organized and running efficiently every day of the year and through all four seasons.

I was also learning how to be a barn manager and how to deal with my boarders under good and bad circumstances. I was learning more about myself then I ever dared to think about. I was slowly trying on many different hats and they were not cowboy hats or helmets of any kind. The hats I was putting on (and some did not fit well at first) had to do with my relationship with my clients and how I handled each situation that came up on our farm.

The Caretaker Hat

If you are going to own a horse business or become a barn manager then once you are deep into the daily grind of life on a farm, you will soon realize that the horses will be the easiest part by far. Learning to take care of horses on a farm is pretty straight forward once you get a system down that works well for your barn. Each farm will be different but when something is working and the horses are happy and healthy you will find that sweet spot and you will know it. It is the best feeling in the world.

The one key factor that is probably one of the most important elements is the fact that if you have horses, be prepared for the unexpected. It will happen and it will catch you off guard and it will always involve the owner of the horse. That can be good and it can be bad. Horses get into everything and the change of weather and seasons can add to all of it. This will keep you on your toes. I love wearing the hat of caretaker of these amazing animals.

The Teacher Hat

Early on in our business I realized that many of our clients were brand new horse owners and they needed some guidance. This was a new area for me and putting on the hat of a teacher was uncomfortable for me in the beginning. I don't like to tell others what to do and at our barn I really believe in letting our boarders do what they want with their horse as long as it is safe for them and the horse.

Soon I was learning how to offer advice and trying to educate my boarders that had questions and needed some help. Having the heart of a teacher is a wonderful thing to have and when you can help someone else that is learning something for the first time, being there for them will open doors and give them confidence to go forward. I believe a good barn manager truly has a heart of a teacher. Years later, I really feel comfortable in this hat and I am honored to wear it.

Having the heart of a teacher is a wonderful thing to have and when you can help someone else that is learning something for the first time, being there for them will open doors and give them the confidence to go forward.

The Enforcer Hat

Another hat I had to put on was the enforcer hat. We have barn rules and they are in place for a reason. Safety is the number one reason but I wanted our barn to stay clean and it is very hard to keep a barn with forty horses clean unless we all do our part and pick up after ourselves. This hat was not fun to wear and it still is not at times but it is a much needed hat.

I still have a hard time reminding someone to pick up their manure in the arena or clean up before they go home but I do it. We have a great group of boarders at our barn and they do a fantastic job but once in a while I need to remind someone about one of our rules and I now accept it is part of the job.

The Medical Hat

You will find yourself wearing the medical hat when a horse gets hurt and you will be the comforter when a horse needs to be put down. You will find yourself wearing these hats often if you have a lot of horses at your barn. Horses get into everything and even though you are not a veterinarian, you will be asked to look at many cuts and abrasions to see if it needs medical attention or if the veterinarian needs to be called. When a horse becomes lame, many times you will be asked to watch the horse as he is moving. It is part of the job and your clients will be asking you for your opinion.

There are also a couple of other hats that are so important and these hats you can choose to wear or not to wear but I think they are vital in making a person complete and well-rounded as a barn manager or owner of any horse business.

The Student Hat

The first hat is the hat of a student. I never knew that I would be learning so much about people and myself through these years of running my own business and it has really made me reflect on myself as a person and who I want to be inside.

When I humble myself and can admit that I have made a mistake to a client, it shows them the respect they deserve and it teaches me how to be a better leader. I believe you will learn more from your mistakes then you will ever learn from never making mistakes at all. Growth as a leader comes from adversity, experience and time. Be ready to learn as a student when a teachable moment happens and watch your leadership skills go through the roof.

Growth as a leader comes from adversity, experience and time. Be ready to learn as a student when a teachable moment happens and watch your leadership skills go through the roof.

The Weatherman Hat

The last hat is the weatherman hat. I know that sounds crazy but read on and you will see what I am talking about. You are going to set the tone for your barn. When you walk in the barn your clients will watch to see what kind of mood you are in. You will either set a positive mood in your barn or a negative mood. You will have your clients either feeling comfortable or walking on egg shells.

You have the power to create a great atmosphere or a place where people wished you stayed in the house and never came out. I am going to admit that there have been a couple of times when I have come into the barn and lost my temper and created a very negative atmosphere. Thank goodness those times have been few and far between but I made it a point to learn from them and be very aware of my moods and behavior.

As the barn owner or manager, you might be having a bad day, but as a professional, you need to keep it together and not take it out on your clients. You can be honest with them and that is fine. But remember, it is a business first and they pay a lot of money to keep their horse at your facility and they come out to relax and enjoy their horse. They should not have to be subjected to your temper or bad mood just because they are in the barn when you are. Be as professional as you can and if you make a mistake and lose it, then apologize. Learn from those times. It is your responsibility to set the tone of the barn. Make it a warm and inviting place to be.

As the barn owner or manager, you might be having a bad day, but as the professional, you need to keep it together and not take it out on your clients.

I have had many people over the years come to me looking for a different place to board their horse and one of the main reasons they want to leave their barn is because the atmosphere is negative and the barn owner is always yelling at everyone. Sometimes it's not the care that is bad. The negative atmosphere of your barn will cause your clients to want to leave.

Be ready for what each day may bring

Each morning I spend a few moments thinking about my day ahead. After many years I am ready for whatever hat I need to wear and I want to wear them with honesty and integrity. If I make a mistake then I will put on my student hat and learn from the situation. I have worn the student hat many times over the years and I am sure I will wear it in the future. Never stop learning.

Behind every successful barn is a knowledgeable, strong and honest barn manager. Learn to be that person and watch your business grow and be all that it can be. Be ready for whatever hat you are asked to wear and even if they are uncomfortable at first, give it a try. You will find yourself putting on each hat with confidence and it will become easier the longer you wear them.

Chapter 11

Fear Can Be the Big Reason Your Barn is Having So Many Problems

Fear can manifest itself in so many ways and we might not even be aware that fear is the underlying force. It can be hard to detect if you are not familiar with the client and it almost never willingly shows itself for what it really is. You have to be creative and do some detective work at times to find out where it is stemming from.

This will be true in your horse business as I learned when we opened our boarding business. I believe successful barn owners can see fear when it presents itself in an angry or upset client and the barn owner will have learned (or will learn) how to dissolve it and replace it with trust.

I have learned so much from my past experiences boarding my horses at many stables growing up in California. Even though at the time many of the things that happened seemed horrible, they molded me and taught me so much and I have carried it into adulthood and into my business.

When I look back at those situations I truly believe they have helped me be a much better barn owner and barn manager. I understand what the boarder is feeling when they are worried that their horse is not going to get fed enough and I also understand the fear they have with putting their horse in with other pasture mates especially if their horse has been the one getting beat up at previous barns.

It is a terrible feeling to come out to the barn and see your horse beat up with fear in his eyes and the barn owner has no place to move him to or worse, refuses to move him when clearly there is a problem. It is a horrible feeling when your horse is losing weight and the barn owner doesn't see a problem or refuses to feed more hay. I have walked down that road and you feel helpless.

You can make a difference

What happens when you become the owner of a boarding facility? You either have the choice to brush off the fears of your clients and not think about it again or you can try your hardest to find out what is the source of their fear and work on a way to build trust. Without trust from your clients your job will be ten times harder and much more complicated.

Fear will show itself in so many ways but one of the most common ways it comes out is in strong opinions from your clients. I have learned over the years that when I talk with a new boarder and they are intense and have very strong opinions, most of the time they are reacting to past bad experiences. After they have been at my barn for a couple of months and they start to see that their horse is getting great care and enough to eat, they become a whole new person that is relaxed and a joy to be around.

Sometimes we miss the opportunity to really get to know the person inside because we never get past the first impression we see when they first move their horse to our barn. If you take the time to really reassure them along the way, you will form a business relationship with them that is built on trust and respect and they will stay and be a devoted client. That to me is what a successful boarding operation looks like.

The reality is that once in a while you will have a client that is just plain difficult because that is their personality. I believe that is not the norm at all. I really believe most people don't want to be difficult at all and they are just trying to protect themselves and their horse.

If you want a barn with low turnover and the most devoted boarders around, take the time to really get to know them. Try to find out what their fears are and give them time to adjust.

Don't let the fear spread

One more thought-Your clients will talk with each other. If they are fearful about the care of their horse, it will soon spread to other people at your barn. This can be very stressful on a barn owner especially when the clients are questioning everything that is done for the care of the horses. If you feel like your barn is out of control then take the time to have a barn meeting and really open up the communication with your boarders and answer the questions they have. The extra work and time you put in during the early years of your business will reap the benefits of having clients that trust you.

As the barn owner it is your responsibility to set the tone for your barn and create an atmosphere built on trust and respect for each other. It might take time but it can happen and when it does, you will notice the positive changes in your barn. The fear will be replaced with trust and then you will know you are on your way to a very successful horse business.

Chapter 12

Why Do So Many Horse Boarding Barns Go Out of Business?

I was talking to a man who I met the other day and we were discussing the horse industry and the area of horse boarding. He has been in the agriculture business for many years and has visited many horse farms in the Midwest area. He was telling me that many of them go out of business after the first couple of years and the reasons were usually always the same. They had poor barn management and business skills.

He went on to tell me that many of these horse boarding facilities were beautiful new barns with many wonderful amenities and so much to offer. These farms had no problem bringing in boarders but they had a big problem keeping them. The turnover was high.

Another common thread to these barns going out of business was the lack of business skills the barn owners had and they would get themselves in over their head with debt and couldn't get out. Most of them didn't have a sound knowledge and healthy grasp on how much it cost to feed all the horses in their care or the other huge expenses it took to run a large horse farm.

After our conversation was over I spent all afternoon thinking about what he had told me and my mind started going back to ten years ago when we built our barn and opened for business. I totally understood what he was talking about because I was there. I was a new barn owner that had zero business skills and really didn't have a grasp on how to run a large horse farm and all the cost that went with it. I did have a business plan that I had to develop for our bank loan and I know that was one of the best things we ever did. That business plan really did open my eyes to so much about the financial side of a working farm.

When I am asked by someone how we have kept our horse boarding business alive even under the worst circumstances in the beginning, my answer is always the same. We learned to run our horse farm as a business and I didn't make the same mistakes twice. I had on the job training every day!

I believe the key to success is not always doing everything right the first time. Successful barns are created from people who make mistakes as they are learning but are willing to change the things that need to be changed and move forward. I believe the reason a barn goes out of business is NOT because there are too many other barns in the area and not enough horses to go around. I believe competition is good for business.

The reason a barn goes out of business is NOT because there are too many other barns in the area and not enough horses to go around. I believe competition is good for business.

If you set your standards high for the daily care of the horses at your farm and run an honest, consistent barn, it will set your business apart. Before you know it your stable will be full and you will have a waiting list.

Today I encourage you to start making the changes at your barn that are hurting your business. If you are just starting out and thinking of building a new barn or have been in the business a few years but still are having problems, find a person that can mentor you through some of the tough issues you are going through and who will give you honest feedback about how your operation is running.

Sometimes all we need is someone from the outside to look at our situation with a fresh pair of eyes to find new opportunities for improvement.

Chapter 13

Growing Pains of a New Business

Every new business is going to have growing pains and the horse industry is no exception. You will hear someone talk about growing pains that a barn is having but until you are living it, you will not fully understand the affect it has on you as the barn owner and the clients at your barn.

When we opened our boarding business I was on cloud nine. I thought we had the perfect business and I was ready to give our boarders whatever they wanted to make them happy. Our barn was a brand new building and I thought it was perfect. I thought our boarders would be happy and stay for years to come. I had a lot to learn about business and people.

Growing pains is hard on your clients

Before we built our barn, we had two people that kept their horses at our farm for a couple of years. They were excited we were building and even helped us a lot during the process. In my mind I didn't think things would change all that much for them once the new barn was built but it turned out to be a much bigger change than we all expected.

These two boarders were used to a quiet farm and no rules. After all how many rules do you need with two boarders? Their board was very low but with the new arena coming and huge mortgage their board was going to increase and I was worried that it might be too much for them.

Within a month our barn was completely full and we were taking care of forty horses seven days a week. It was a very busy barn and people were here all the time. Very quickly into the first few months I found myself in unfamiliar territory of trying to fulfill many special requests at our barn. We also were cleaning stalls seven days a week which was starting to make me extremely tired. Our days were long and our barn hours were much longer than they are now.

Our two boarders that had helped us so much during the building process had some big adjustments also. The tack room that they used was now very crowded with quite a few other people and tack. They now didn't have the freedom to choose whatever stall they wanted to use in our small barn anymore.

They were used to bringing their dogs to our farm because we only had four horses but now I had a new rule that no dogs were allowed in the barns or arenas at all. With forty horses and many people it would be crazy if everyone brought their dogs so we said "no dogs" at the farm except on a leash and they had to stay outside away from all horses and barns. That didn't go over well.

I also had to increase their board and now I needed to charge sales tax which added on quite a bit and they were not happy about this. It all started to catch up with them and it became stressful at times. We were experiencing growing pains and it was very painful for all of us and it put a strain on our friendship.

The way things look on paper seem so clear and clean cut but once you have horses in the barn and people everywhere things can become very foggy very fast. I was letting our boarders do pretty much whatever they wanted to do and I didn't have barn rules set up yet. I couldn't think of many rules because I didn't see what could go wrong!

Out of control

People were helping themselves to as much hay as they wanted and we were wasting hay in large amounts. People were not cleaning up after themselves and not cleaning up after their horse. Drama was a huge problem in our barn and I had boarders that wanted to leave because our barn was becoming a very negative place to be. I had people that were using other people's tack and even their stall if they wanted. Respect had gone out the window for some people and it became a free for all. I knew it was time for some big changes.

We were a very new business and David and I were not business people at all. When I think back to those first couple of years, I must say they are a blur and a terrible time for me. When business owners talk about growing pains it doesn't necessary mean that the business is growing larger.

When the barn owner starts to change

Many times growing pains happen in a barn because the barn owners are changing and becoming business people. Their eyes have been opened to many things that need to change and be corrected for the betterment of the business. When this happens it is very good for the barn owners but many times the clients have a hard time adjusting mainly because they are not able to do whatever they want anymore. We were no exception.

As David and I started evolving into business owners I started making changes in the barn that some of our boarders didn't like. Basically I was becoming a leader and once I started to lead and establish rules, they were not able to be the leader anymore and it caused some friction. During these times of redirection and growing as business owners we lost a few boarders. They left for others barns that better suited them.

Growing pains in a young business is very common and it will come in many forms. Growing pains can come when your business changes or grows and the clients that were there from the beginning have a hard time adjusting to a new way of doing things.

Growing pains also happen a lot as you try to figure out what works and what doesn't at your farm. This can go on for a few years in any business. Our growing pains lasted for about three years!

Whether you are dealing with people and barn rules or changing the layout of your paddocks because you realize the design does not work well, you will have changes. Some barns will go through many changes in their first few years and some might only have a few changes but they are all growing pains of running your business. When you are making these changes it might not sit well with all your clients and you need to be prepared for this.

People don't always like change

People don't like change and many reasons a new business loses so many clients in the first couple of years is because people don't want to hang around while you figure everything out. You will have some that will stay (we also had boarders that stayed through all the changes) but be prepared and don't take it personally if some of your boarders leave during these times. The element of the unknown is always scary to people and when you make a change, no one really knows how it is going to turn out until it has proven either good or bad.

Keep the communication open

I encourage you to talk with your boarders and keep the communication open both ways. If they have a concern during changes at your barn then take the time to talk with them. Listen to their thoughts and reassure them that it will be okay. Be honest with them and let them know you are making changes to better your barn for the horses and the clients. The more honest you are with why you are making changes the more likely they are to stay on during this time of growth.

One of the biggest mistakes I made in our early years was the lack of communication on my part. I was dealing with strong personalities at my barn and I had zero confidence as a barn owner. I tried my best to talk with them but looking back I did a poor job of communicating because I didn't have confidence in myself as a barn owner and leader.

Growing pains will help you grow inside

Growing pains will affect your clients but it will also greatly affect you, the barn owner. I want you to look at growing pains as a positive part of becoming a business person and they will help you move toward having a successful horse business. They may not be easy to go through but you will grow inside as you are making changes and moving forward.

If you don't have growing pains then there is nothing to prompt you to better yourself and the business you have created. Take those pains you are feeling and act on them and turn the situation into something even better. If you do this you will be pleasantly surprised at how your business will improve and you will start to feel yourself change and grow into the business person you know you are inside.

If you don't have growing pains then there is nothing to prompt you to better yourself and the business you have created. Take those pains you are feeling and act on them and turn the situation into something even better.

Chapter 14

The Many Changes You Will Make in the Early Years

Change is part of everything in life and your equine business will have its share of them over the years. We made many changes during the first three years of our business and now after many years of boarding horses we still make changes now and then.

It would be safe to say that the largest changes happen early on in any business but as your business grows and evolves, so do you. I believe positive change at times is healthy for a business and those changes can take place at any time in your equine career.

The one thing I want to make very clear is there is a huge difference between making changes and lack of consistency. Making a change in a specific area of your horse business is usually a onetime change and if it works well then it doesn't get changed again for a long time.

There is a huge difference between making changes and a lack of consistency.

The lack of consistency is where you do one thing one day and change it the next and then change it again the next day. It never stays the same. Your clients don't know what to expect when this happens and it will be very stressful for them. Many barns have problems because they can't keep their barn chores consistent and the boarders see this.

I have talked with potential boarders that come to our barn for a tour and one of the reasons they want to leave the barn they are currently at is because they don't know when their horse is going to be fed each day. I have heard horror stories where one day their horse is fed at 6am and the next morning they are fed at 10am. They tell me that they are not sure if their horse is even getting their grain on a daily basis and the amount they are supposed to be fed is never the same. Those are two great examples of inconsistency and those are the things that will ruin a barn's reputation.

Over the years we have made some huge changes and many smaller ones. Even this last year I made a couple of small changes and our boarders rolled with it. I truly believe my boarders handle our changes quite well because they trust us and know that we will always put the horses first.

Once your boarders know and believe that you run a consistent barn on a daily basis, the changes you make will not faze them so much because they will trust you all the way through it.

Changes in riding disciplines

Many of the changes you will make will have to do with your clientele at the time. We are a multi-discipline barn and when we first opened our doors we had a large number of dressage and saddle seat riders. These types of riders will use the arena in a different way than other disciplines and we had to adjust during our peak hours of riding time.

Now we have more people that want to jump and very little saddle seat and dressage riders at our barn. Because we have so many people that jump it involves putting the jumps up and it does take up more of the arena. We now have jump standards out in our back arena year round and if it is winter time then everyone needs to be very open to sharing our indoor arena and communication is a vital part of making it all work. No matter what the discipline or time of year, communication is important.

Many changes will happen

We have changed our barn hours and actually shortened them. We changed stall cleaning from seven days a week to six days a week and our grain program has changed dramatically over the years. I have changed our rules several times over the years depending on what was happening at the time. I have added rules and even taken away rules that we no longer needed. I have changed our late payment schedule from a ten day grace period to a five day grace period and I have made changes in what I charge for extra services and what I will include for free. The list can go on and on but the changes I have made over the years have only bettered our barn and made my life much easier.

If you find yourself becoming stressed out over situations that keep recurring then it might be time to make some changes that will make things easier for everyone at the barn. The changes you make will many times benefit you and equally important they will benefit your clients.

The one thing I want you to remember is that the changes you make will not always be popular with all your clients. Change is hard for some and if the changes you are making are a result of an issue then there might be a chance that not everyone will be pleased. That is okay and you need to remember that the business comes first and you have to do what is best for your business, family and ultimately your life.

Making changes for your family

When we changed our barn hours after our first year it was upsetting for a few people that liked to come out to our barn late in the evening. David and I were exhausted and it was hard for us to go to bed if we knew people were riding in the arena late at night. It made for a very long day for us. When we changed our barn hours to an earlier closing time during the school year, there were a few that didn't like the change but we needed to make the change for us as a family.

Many of the changes you make will be because you need to balance out your business with your personal life and family. If you are running a barn and living on the same property your life will be entwined with the business every day of the year and it is very hard to separate the two at times. Some of the changes you make will be made solely for your personal and family life. If you listen closely to what your body is telling you there will be signs that is time to make a change. Don't burn yourself out as many barn owners do. There will be many times when you put your clients first and then there will be times that you need to put yourself and your family first and that might involve change.

I encourage you today to take time to reevaluate your business and how it affects you and your family. Look at how it runs every day and if there are things you can do to make the barn run smoother then try them. You won't regret it and you will find many times that it is better for your clients and yourself. Your business needs change to grow and become exceptional and so do you. All these little things you go through during these times of change will set you apart as a barn owner/manager and it will set your horse business apart from the rest.

Chapter 15

It's a Working Farm

Let me start off by saying that your boarders will from time to time forget that your farm is a working farm. They will forget that the hay needs to be delivered and stacked and during the summer there are going to be tractors coming and going. They will forget that the grass needs to be cut and the snow needs to be plowed. Everything that needs to be done on a farm to keep it going will be done throughout the year and it will include loud equipment of many types.

When we first opened our business my husband tried his very hardest to do things when the boarders were not out riding. He would wait until late at night to plow snow so he didn't have to do it while they were at the barn and even cut grass early in the morning around the barn and arena so he didn't upset the boarders. Now looking back, the horses always did just fine with the sound of the tractors and equipment. Usually it was the people that were more upset than the horses.

Enough is enough

David was slowly killing himself trying to do so many maintenance jobs after hours and we finally came to a point where we had to say enough was enough. He started doing the things that needed to get done like plowing snow during the day and it became so much easier for him. He would let the boarders know when he was going to be plowing around the barn to remove snow that had fallen off of the roof and then after that, it was their choice if they wanted to ride or not.

We had to stop tip toeing around all our clients and they had to realize that is was a working farm. In order to keep barns full of hay and shavings and the driveway free from snow and ice, work needed to get done and it was going to be done during the day even if people were riding.

You wouldn't think that this even needs to be addressed but if you are going to run a boarding barn then you will no doubt have a client now and then that will be very nervous about handling their horse unless it is completely quiet. The fear that the horse will spook and something will happen can cause them to be very anxious. Unless they get over that fear and let their horse get used to the noise of a tractor or snowplow, they will have problems wherever they go. All barns have work that needs to get done and they all use some sort of large equipment to do it.

Educating helps

Your boarders will never understand all that it takes to run a farm and you have to be okay with that. Education and communication are important in helping your clients understand barn operations and most of the time you won't have any problems.

When I boarded my horses I never gave any thought to what it took to keep the boarding stable going. I just came out and rode. That is what most people do and you can't fault them for that. You can educate them so they will understand your rules and operations and they might really appreciate it.

We have such a fantastic group of boarders at our barn now and many of them understand that we have a working farm and they will ask me questions from time to time about all the things that need to be done behind the scenes of our farm. The best part is many of them want to help and they have been a blessing for us when the hay comes in and needs to be unloaded or the grass needs to get cut.

Take time to talk with your boarders and you will find that many of them would love to be part of the big picture of a working horse farm. When this happens you will have a great team right there ready to help with anything that needs to get done. Let them get involved and be part of your working farm and the blessings will come for all involved.

Chapter 16

Is Your Barn Designed for Horses or People?

Our barn was built in 2005 and it is extremely practical. It is very large but nothing fancy. We don't have a heated barn (even though I wish we did during the winter) but our indoor arena allows for people to ride year round.

Many people have come to our farm for a tour of our facility because they want to build a barn of their own. I usually hear the same response each time that our barn is very practical and built with the horse in mind. The word fancy never comes up when talking about our barn but well designed for horses is mentioned a lot. Are there things I would like to change now that we have been in business and both horses and people use it every day? Sure there are.

I absolutely love to walk through other barns and it is safe to say I would rather take a tour of a barn then go through a tour of homes any day. I have been through many barns and now that I own and run a large barn I look at things in a much different way. I look at barns from a functional point of view.

The functional barn

Is the air ventilation good for the horses both during the summer and winter? Is it extremely warm in the barn on those hot days of summer? Is it easy to hang fans safely without a horse chewing on the cord? How easy is it to water the horses and feed hay? Are the stalls big enough for a very large horse? Where is the tack room compared to where you are going to tack up? Is it easy to walk your horse down the aisle and move around other horses safely? Where are the electric outlets for clipping and for the veterinarian and farrier? Is there easy access to brooms, shovels, muck buckets and wheelbarrows to keep the barn clean as much as possible? When stalls are cleaned is it easy to dump the wheelbarrow? As you can see the list can go on and on.

Sometimes a barn will be designed for the comfort of the people that own the horses but that is not always the best for the horses that live in the barn. There are many different ways to design a barn and if you are in the middle of designing your barn, I encourage you to go to as many farms as you can and ask to tour them. Ask the barn owners what works and what doesn't work. Ask them what they would do different if they could build over. Find out if they have a problem with snow removal in the wintertime or flooding in the spring.

So many things look good on paper but once you are using them on a daily basis it is easy to see the flaws and what needs to be changed. Build your barn for the health of the horse first and your boarders will adjust to how you have it designed.

Look at the big picture

If you are in the boarding business long enough you will have clients that will ask you to change things now and then to make it easier for them. When this happens you need to look at the big picture and how it will affect all of the horses in the barn. It could be something like putting lights in a stall for the coat of the horse. Some people like lights on their horse so they don't grow a long winter coat. If you don't have solid walls between horses the lights might affect other horses in the nearby stalls.

We had this issue years ago when a couple of boarders wanted to put special lighting up in their stalls for their horse's coats. The lights shined into their stall and also the stalls on both sides of their horses. The lights were bright and this upset the boarders that owned horses in the stalls next door. We finally said "no" to lights in the stalls. Depending on the breed and habits of the show circuit for that breed, you might be asked to change things in your barn. We have been asked to keep horses in twenty-four hours a day because this was common in some circles of showing. With this request the horses would never go outside at all and we felt it was not a good fit for us at the time. I always tell people design your barn for the horse and design the lounge for the people and all will be happy!

Design your barn for the horse and design the lounge for the people and all will be happy!

Don't forget your boarders

Remember that when you are designing your barn, think about the functionality of it and how it will affect your boarders. If the muck buckets, picks and shovels are in an area that is inconvenient or far away, there is a good chance your boarders will not clean up as often as you would like. You need to make it easy for them to get at everything.

If the trash can is down at the other end of the barn, they are not going to want to walk all the way down there to throw something away. Put a few garbage cans out and your barn will stay cleaner. If the hose to water the horses is extremely hard to use and not in a good location your employees might not do the best job of filling buckets. You can hope they will but if everything is hard when doing chores it will take longer and it will end up costing you more money.

If you are going to have grooming stalls, try to make a couple of them to get horses out of the way of the aisle when people are brushing and tacking up horses. It greatly helps with congestion and keeps people and horses a safer.

These suggestions all may seem a trivial but I guarantee once you are in full operation and your barn is full of horses and people, you will start to notice things you can do to make your barn better for the horses that live there and the people that use your barn.

I am always trying to improve our barn and even the little things that make horse care more convenient for the boarders are a plus. A barn should be a healthy and positive place for both the horse and their owner.

Chapter 17

Barn Hours Are Important!

If you don't think barn hours are important then you have not had enough time running your own boarding facility. When you decide to start boarding horses on your property you will no doubt be just like I was many years ago. I was so excited to be able to work at home and take care of horses. To me there was no better job and I thought I was living the dream.

When we first opened our barn our hours were from 8am to 10pm every day of the week. I had an endless amount of energy and 10pm seemed very reasonable. We opened in the summer and it stayed light until about 9pm so closing at 10pm was pretty easy in the beginning.

As the days became shorter and the sun went down earlier my days became much longer and I started to become exhausted. We were out in the barn each morning very early and I was having a very hard time staying awake until 10pm to close the barn down. My husband David would be the one that would go out to the barn and top off the water buckets and close the barn down most of the time but he was becoming extremely tired also.

Our barn opened at 8am every day and people would be there as it opened. Our barn closed at 10pm every day and there would be boarders riding all the way up to 10pm every night. After they would leave we would go in the barn to check and make sure all the lights were off and all the stalls were latched. It never failed we would find lights on and even a stall partly open once in a while. Things were not put away and David and I found ourselves cleaning up after our boarders at 10:30 at night which was crazy!

I know that many boarding barns have late riding hours and it works for them but for us it became very stressful especially when we would walk in the barn and find a stall door open with the horse still inside for the time being. We knew we needed to make some changes when it came to our barn hours but we were a new business and I was worried we were going to lose boarders over the change.

I decided to first write a letter to all our boarders and explain the importance of cleaning up after themselves and making sure the stall doors are closed completely and all the lights are off. I even went as far as to explain that David and I went into the barn each night to check and make sure all the horses were safely in their stall and that we had found stalls that were not safety latched at all. I talked about the importance of cleaning up and making sure everything was put away.

A few more months passed by and things really didn't get any better. I believe our boarders tried to do what was right but they were usually in a hurry at closing time and that's when things were left unattended.

A few months later we decided to change our closing hours to 8pm during the school year and 9pm during the summer months. It was a scary decision to make and I know it didn't please a few people that worked late but I had to do what was best for David and me and our family. We made the change and moved forward. I couldn't believe what a difference it made in our life to close the barn at 8pm during the winter when it was dark and cold outside. It was truly one of the best changes we have ever made for our family.

Find what hours work best for you

Many barns are going to have different hours depending on where you live. If you live in a hot state like Arizona then most people will ride early in the morning or late in the evening to beat the heat of the day. If you live in the Midwest where the days are very short and cold in the winter, not many people ride after dark and so for that reason having early closing hours will work.

Finding what works best for your barn is a completely individual choice. If you have employees that can close the barn down at night then you don't need to worry. If you are more like David and me where you are the ones that do all the work and close the barn down each night, then you will need to think about what works best for you.

Your hours will fit their schedule

Barns hours will be very important to some people that work late but I believe that once you set your barn hours the right people will come and your hours will be a perfect fit for their schedule. Don't be disappointed if your barn hours don't work for every potential boarder. If you are running a barn with great care the right boarders will find you and many times they will adjust their schedule to fit your barn hours. They will do this because they know you will take great care of their horse and that is the most important thing to them.

Over the last year I have talked with several barn owners that have burned themselves out and for a number of reasons. One of the big ones is because they don't want to change their barn hours. They are worried they are going to lose clients and they won't take a chance. They complain about how tired they are and that they have people at their farm at five in the morning and as late at midnight riding and then when something goes wrong they are called out to the barn to fix the problem no matter what time it is. Believe me it happens more than you know.

If you don't want a call at midnight then don't keep your barn open till midnight. It is as straight forward as that.

Setting barn hours is healthy for your barn

Setting barn hours is a healthy part of barn management and even though we live in a world that never sleeps, don't let that happen at your farm. The horses need time to rest without people there and lights on. They need quiet time and even though the world has become a very busy place, their world is still the same. They do so much better when there is a schedule and a time to rest without human intervention.

As a barn owner you will find out in the first year what is going to work and not work for you when it comes to your barn hours. It doesn't matter what other barns are doing and how late they stay open. All that matters is what works for your barn, business and family. Remember, give great care and your boarders will stay even if you have to make a change in the hours at your barn.

Chapter 18

Private Turnout vs. Group Turnout

If you have ever looked at boarding facilities and what they offer, you will find out very fast that each one has a little something different to offer when it comes to turnout.

I am going to start off by saying there is not a right way or wrong way to have turnout for horses. Most boarding barns in the area where I live offer group turnout with private turnout for an extra fee. A friend of mine that lives in another state only offers individual turnout for the horses at her barn and it works great for her.

My barn offers group turnout of no more than six horses in a herd and it works out well for the size of our paddocks and pastures. We also have a few paddocks for private turnout because if you have horses then you will likely have one or two that end up on the injured reserve list and need private turnout to heal. We have also had a few show horses that are on private turnout during show season.

There are barns that have a large number of horses in each herd and there are barns that have herds of only two or three. There are many ways to set up your barn and herd turnout for the horses in your care and there are pros and cons to each of them.

Group Turnout

The benefits of group turnout are many. Horses are herd animals and they enjoy being around other horses. Even if they don't get along with every horse in their herd they will stick together for the most part. Very few horses like to be alone. Herd turnout is good for them mentally because it gets them moving and the stimulation they get from playing and touching each other is healthy for them. When our horses have been outside for the day they come in relaxed and content. They have spent the day doing what horses do and you can see they are happy.

There are a few negatives for group turnout. If you are going to show your horse there is a chance that he might come in with a few nips here and there especially if he likes to play. We have a couple groups of geldings that play constantly and once in a while one of them will come in with some hair missing. With group turnout you also take the chance of horses getting into it and leaving kick or bite marks on each other. It is the way of the horse and how they communicate and even the closest of horses can have a bad day with each other.

Group turnout sometimes is not a good fit for the very senior horse or a horse that has some physical disabilities. It can put them at risk and once a horse reaches a certain age it is really time to look at a quieter paddock with only one or possibly two other very quiet horses to live with.

The herds and the client

As the barn owner you need to remember that however you design your paddocks for your herds will also have an impact on the owner of each horse. They will come to you with many questions especially if they are a new horse owner. If a horse is getting beat up you will hear about it and need to have an educated answer for the owner.

Safety issues with herd turnout and the client

Group turnout is something that many people are not familiar with and when they want to get their horse out of the herd, some of them might have a few problems if the other horses crowd them when they walk into the paddock. It can be intimidating to the new horse owner or a person that does not have confidence.

If you board horses long enough you will find yourself educating many boarders on how to safely get their horse out of the paddock without getting hurt or letting the other horses out through the gate. I have seen both happen because the owner was not sure how to handle all the horses that surround them when they go out to get their horse.

There has been a few times over the years where a boarder was trying to get their horse out of the paddock and another raced through the gate at the same time and then I hear the dreaded words, "Loose Horse!" I don't panic like I used to because the loose horse rarely leaves the others but I can't relax until I know he is caught and safe.

Educating your boarders will be part of your job when it comes to herds and safely getting their horse out of the paddock.

Private Turnout

Private turnout for horses also has some pros and cons. Private turnout is a necessity to have if you are going to run a boarding barn. You will most likely have horses that injure themselves and need to heal in a quieter place than a group setting.

Horses that are hurt don't think about reinjuring themselves as they are tearing across the field after another horse. I have seen many people turn their horse out with a herd far too soon because they, "Feel sorry" for them. It always ends up bad and the horse begins his long recovery on stall rest again all because the owner wanted him out with the herd sooner than he should have been.

One reason people don't put their horse on private turnout is because at most boarding facilities private turnout is an extra fee. At our barn we charge so much per day for private turnout and that is the norm with many places. Private turnout is more work for the barn owner and if it is not part of your normal board amenities, it should cost extra.

Some will spend, some will not

You will find people that will gladly pay for private turnout and others that don't want to spend the extra money. Sometimes it is better to spend a few extra dollars and have a strong recovery than to try and save money and end up with another vet bill because you put your horse back in the herd too soon. As the barn owner, you will see every scenario and you will be the one that has to figure out what is best in each situation.

Private turnout is great for the elderly horse that has become fragile and needs a quiet space to live during the day. It is also a great thing to offer for people that show horses and want their horses coat to stay bite free.

I have also seen horses that don't do well on private turnout. Some horses are on private turnout because the owner is worried that something will happen in the herd setting. In this situation once in a while the horse will pick up vices due to boredom or stress. You will need to treat each one of these situations on an individual basis and I can promise you that no two situations will ever be the same.

We had one horse years ago that was young and kept getting hurt in the herd he was in. We moved him to a couple different herds trying to find a place that best suited him and in each herd he would come out with new marks and he even needed stitches a few times. Finally after a frustrating six months the owners decided to pay for private turnout. One day I went out to get him and bring him in for the evening and he was limping with a huge cut on his leg. I couldn't believe it and neither could the owners. We looked everywhere to see where he could have hurt himself and we never did find anything. Here he was all by himself and he managed to get hurt.

The owners were very upset and gave their notice. I believe deep down inside they thought that our place was unsafe or unfit to keep a horse. I was crushed and very hurt. About a year later I ran into those people at a show and when I saw their horse I noticed his back leg was wrapped. It turned out he had gotten hurt at the barn he was currently boarded at and had to have stitches on his leg. He was going to be okay and I found myself walking away and relieved inside because I knew it was not my place. It was the horse.

When designing, think about private turnout

If I could offer any advice, when creating your layout for the horses that are going to live on your property take an area and build some private turnouts. You will need them for many different situations and without private turnout your job will be much tougher at times. You never know what is going to happen to a horse or what an owner is going to want for turnout. Private turnout will be a great asset to your farm and business and you will make extra money at the same time.

Having different options is essential for a horse boarding business and that includes group and private turnout. If you take the time and put the extra work into making a few more paddocks for private turnout you will never regret it. Our private paddocks get used every day here on our farm and I am glad we have them.

Chapter 19

The Multi-Discipline Barn

I was so fortunate to own a horse growing up. I lived in Los Angeles, California, and most people did not have enough acreage to have horses on their property in that area so boarding was the only option. I was no exception. We boarded my horse at many places during my youth and with every place came many different disciplines of riding. I saw every style of riding and I loved it. It opened my eyes to all that you could do on a horse.

Many years later when we decided to open our boarding barn, there was no question that I wanted a multi-discipline barn. I was hoping to attract many people that owned different breeds and life would be good. Little did I know I was in a learning experience about being the owner of a multi-discipline barn.

We opened for business and the horses came. We had Quarter horses and Thoroughbreds, Warm bloods and Miniature horses and everything in-between. We had western riders, hunt seat riders and the hunter/jumper group. Dressage and saddle seat riders came and also carts both large and small. We had people that loved to show for fun and then people that took it very seriously and competed at a higher level. We had others that preferred trail riding and people that hardly rode but just came out to enjoy being around their horse. It was truly a great mix of people and horses.

Everything started off great that first summer but within a few months problems and issues started taking shape. Let me start off by saying we have a huge indoor arena. It is 80 x 200 which allows for many riders at the same time. At the time we also had a smaller outdoor arena but during the cold and rainy months in Wisconsin, it is very hard to ride outside.

By the time summer was over and we were into autumn I started getting complaints from several people that there were problems in the indoor arena. We had riders that wanted to jump and needed the jump standards out and dressage riders that needed the entire arena to practice their dressage test. We had saddle seat riders that needed the rail and trail riders that wanted to set up a trail course. Then I had a couple of people that wouldn't ride if the ponies came in with the carts. It seemed like everyone wanted everything up at the same time and people were becoming irritated with each other.

At the time I didn't understand why this was becoming an issue and I really didn't know how to fix it. Our arena was huge and there really weren't that many people using it at the same time. When I think about it now, I realize that it wasn't everyone that was complaining. It was just a couple of people who I believe had the "All about me" syndrome and they felt they shouldn't have to deal with anyone else while they were using the arena.

Because I was not a strong leader back then I was running around trying to put out these little fires because I had a couple of riders that were extremely high maintenance. When they rode they didn't want any interruption and I believe they were not used to having to share an arena with anyone.

I even had riders that were telling others they couldn't come in the arena until they were done using it. This angered people very much because they worked and only had a short time to ride to begin with. At that point if I didn't fix the problem as soon as possible they were going to move their horses. I was starting to feel the stress of running a barn and dealing with people.

Time to fix the issues

The first thing I did was send out a letter to all our boarders and explain the importance of respecting each other's space in the arena and I did designate a time each week so the people that wanted to set up a jump course could set up a full one for a couple hours that day and practice. I also had to stress that there was absolutely no telling others that they could not use the arena. Then I had to talk with the people that were causing the problems and dominating the arena which was extremely difficult but needed to be done. This was definitely unfamiliar territory for me as a new barn owner/manager and it was not easy.

We made some new guidelines for using the arena and put them in place. The trail riders would use half the arena if they wanted to set up a practice course and the arena was big enough for others to ride on the other half. After I started taking charge as a barn owner, people started working out their problems in the arena and started sharing it without issues.

To this day we still have a multi-discipline barn and we don't have any of the issues we had back then. People have learned that they need to communicate with each other and if you see someone is jumping then you need to ride around them and give them space.

Once in a while I still need to talk with someone if they decide to set up a trail course and use the entire length of the arena but now I just ask them to move some of the obstacles to one end and it leaves plenty of room for the other riders.

We are lucky because we do have a very large arena which allows for so much flexibility. Your situation might be different especially if you have a small arena. If your arena is smaller and crowded then you will need to talk with your boarders and set up a schedule for some of the riders that use jumps or trail course obstacles. The important thing is communication. Talk with your boarders and ask them about ways to improve the arena atmosphere while in the arena. Ask them to be part of the program to make it better.

No bossy boarders

As a boarding barn, you will always have a couple people that will not be happy with how you set up your arena. To keep a barn healthy and free from a negative atmosphere you need to let your boarders know you are not going to tolerate anyone bossing another person around. You need to do what is in the best interest of the entire barn and if you have a boarder that leaves because they are not happy then you need to be okay with that.

Remember, if someone is not on board with sharing time in the arena and they are the one that is causing so many problems, then it will be better if they move to a barn that better suits their needs and personality.

You have the ability as the barn owner to decide what is allowed and not allowed at your barn and the sooner you let your boarders know you are in charge, the faster things will settle down.

You have the ability as the barn owner to decide what is allowed and not allowed at your barn and the sooner you let your boarders know you are in charge, the faster things will settle down.

Be flexible as your barn changes

One more thought-be flexible as your barn changes. With a boarding barn you will have horses and people come and go and with that will come the change of riding disciplines. When we first opened we had a lot of dressage riders and saddle seat riders and now we have much less. We definitely have more hunt seat and western riders now and so the arena is used in a different way much of the time.

Things never stay the same and you need to be ready for issues that will come up as your clients change. The good news is the longer you run a boarding barn the easier it will become. You will be able to resolve issues much faster and with much less stress because it will be nothing new that you haven't seen before. It does get easier!

Chapter 20

Renting and Sub-Leasing Your Stalls

Keeping your stalls filled and rented is a priority for every person that boards horses. After all that is how you pay your bills each month. I have talked with many barn owners and renting out stalls is handled differently in many barns.

Some barns offer a multi-horse discount and others offer a discount or rate increase depending on the size of the horse. Some barns offer different rates depending on if the stall has a window or not and many barns offer individual turnout with each stall. There are also different rates depending on the size of the stall. Many barns will offer two different size stalls.

There is no right or wrong way to charge for your stalls as long as you are making a profit. After all if you are not charging enough and you are losing money than there is a very good chance you will eventually go out of business.

You will regret setting your rates too low

Many barn owners offer special deals depending on each person's situation and it can get pretty complicated if you allow it. In the long run I don't believe it is good for business. Setting your rates for each stall can be tricky and if you start off too low to attract clients there is a good chance you will regret it in the long run.

When we were building our barn I decided that I was going to charge a different rate for the stalls that had a window. The difference in price was ten dollars per stall and I didn't realize how much I would regret that decision about six months into it. We really didn't know what our finances were going to look like early on and it became a financial struggle quickly without the added income. Later on as boarders left I started charging the same price for all our stalls and it worked out much better for us financially.

Multi-Horse Discount

We have several families that own two or more horses at our barn. I am often asked by potential new boarders if we offer a multi-horse discount and that is something we have never done. I have often wanted to as a perk for people that own more than one horse but our finances would not allow it and you need to keep this in mind if you are thinking about offering a multi-horse discount. The goal is to make money and if you are losing money because you offer a multi-horse discount then you will soon regret it.

You need to remember that even if one family boards several horses at your barn, it will still cost you the same per horse in labor, hay, shavings and everything else. The work load is still the same and they still eat the same amount of hay. I only tell other barn owners that want to offer a multi-horse discount to do it if they are sound financially and they can afford to offer a nice perk to their boarders. Don't do it just to attract clients! You will regret it in the long run. You can't run a business by trying to be nice and offering a multi-horse discount. It doesn't work especially when you are just starting out and money is tight.

The most important thing to keep in mind is that if you are taking great care of the horses and you keep a clean and safe barn, people will pay to be at your barn and the multi-horse discount won't matter at all. We have never offered a discount and we have several families with two and three horses at our barn.

If you are taking great care of the horses and you keep a clean safe barn, people will pay to be at your barn and the multi-horse discount won't matter at all.

When a client should pay more

I do think if you are going to offer two different size stalls then you should charge a different price according to the size of the stall. The same would be true for stalls that have attached run-ins. Those are perks that the client should pay for.

The fear many barn owners have is that they won't be able to fill their stalls and then they won't be able to pay their bills. This is very real and I have felt that same fear go through my body every time someone gives me a thirty day notice.

A good thing when they see it

Just remember that once you earn a great reputation for fantastic care, that will outweigh any discount that you don't give. Remember that most of your boarders have boarded at many other barns and they know what is out there already. They know a good thing when they see it and if you are giving the best care around then they will come with ten horses even if you don't offer a multi-horse discount.

Sub-leasing your stall

I had never thought about a client wanting to sub-lease their stall while their horse was away at training but very early on after we opened I had my first request to sub-lease a stall and it was a learning experience to say the least.

A horse was going down to Florida for training for three months and the owner didn't want to lose their stall. They told me that they had a friend that could come and use the stall for winter because they didn't have an indoor arena where they were boarding. They asked me if it was okay and immediately I said yes not knowing what could go wrong.

Soon the horse left our barn for Florida and the new horse came. I quickly realized that I needed to find a paddock that would be a good fit for this horse and so my job began. The new horse that came in was a little difficult and it took some time to find a herd that worked. After a few weeks everything settled down and I was told the other horse was doing good down in Florida. In the meantime the owners of the new horse that came to our barn for three months sub-leased out their stall at their regular barn.

After about a month I received a call from the people that owned the horse down in Florida. The horse was having some trouble and they wanted to bring him back home where they could follow how his training was going with a trainer in our area. They contacted the person that was sub-leasing the stall at my barn and told them the situation. Then the next in line had to be contacted at the other place. Everything became very complicated overnight and soon there were upset people because the person that was here at my barn didn't want to leave so soon. They thought they had the stall for three months and now everyone was going to change again. It felt like we were playing musical stalls and it was hard on the horses involved and the friendship between those people became strained.

Several other times within the next couple of years I have said yes to sub-leasing a stall and each time it became much more work than it is was worth. People can have the best of intentions but things don't always turn out the way you planned and someone gets hurt.

No more sub-leasing

Finally I decided absolutely no sub-leasing out a stall. If you send your horse away for training, you still need to pay full board for the stall while you are gone. I had one very nice man who boarded a horse at our barn, send his mare away for training for six months and he paid full board at our barn. I told him upfront what the policy was and he was fine with it.

Sub-leasing seems like a great idea but it will always be more work for the barn owner or manager. Whether it is adjusting a new horse to a herd or answering questions and getting the new boarders situated, it is a lot of work for a short period of time.

Many barns sub-lease and it is definitely a personal choice. I don't believe it will hurt your business at all if you don't allow a client sub-lease their stall. If you want offer that to your boarders then make sure you get all the details of when a horse is leaving and when a horse is coming back and get it in writing so that people can't change their mind mid-way through the lease. It will save you much stress if you do it right to begin with.

Chapter 21

Has Your Tack Room Become Too Small?

You can tell that someone is truly horse crazy when they love to walk into a tack room and smell the leather. I love saddles and bridles and brushes for horses. I would rather go to a tack store then go clothes shopping at the mall. Most horse crazy people are the same way. There is something about a tack store that makes us feel good inside and it is very hard to leave without buying lots of goodies.

We have two very large tack rooms in our big barn and a similar size tack room in our small barn. When we built our tack rooms I wanted to make sure we had plenty of space so we opted out of two extra stalls to make room for larger tack rooms.

When our barn opened for business and the boarders came with their tack it was more stuff then I ever imagined. Overnight our tack rooms were filled up. I had a few clients that owned just a tack box and a few other necessities along with their saddle and bridle. Then I had clients that had more stuff then I had room for in the tack room. I had people bring tack chests and many cabinets and I even had one person ask if she could bring an armoire! When she told me the dimensions I knew it wouldn't fit in our tack room and she asked if she could keep it out in the barn aisle. I was shocked to say the least. I told her that she couldn't bring it and she would need to find something smaller!

Put a limit on it

Over the years I have seen pretty much everything that a person can buy for horses end up at our barn and in the tack room. I finally had to be assertive and put a limit on what a boarder could have for space. I must admit that when we opened our barn years ago I was so overwhelmed by everything else that the tack rooms were the last thing on my mind. After all I was dealing with many adults and they should be able to share and not crowd others out. I was surprised at how many calls I received early on because I had boarders that were very upset because they hardly had any room. Someone else was crowding them out with all their stuff and it was causing issues between people in all three of our tack rooms.

I have found out since those early years that it is much easier and far better to give everyone a designated space and put a limit on it right from the first day they arrive. If they know how much room they have for their things you don't have to come back and try to solve issues later.

If you give some people as much room as they want, I can guarantee that they will fill every space available. That is fine if you only have a few boarders but if you are running a large barn with many people, things can get out of hand quickly and before you know it your tack room is going to be full and a mess.

I rarely go into the boarders tack rooms anymore. Our boarders are great about keeping it clean and putting things in their place. Once in a while David and I will go in to clean and I will put a few things away but for the most part everything has its place and I don't get any more calls from angry boarders.

Designate an area for each person

If I can give a few words of advice-give everyone a designated area for their tack and belongings. Be very clear about what you allow in the tack room. We don't allow any dirty blankets at all in any of the tack rooms. They smell and they create more of a mess because of everything that is on them. If a boarder is done using their blankets after winter, the blankets must go home. After the blankets have been washed then they can bring them back to store them in the tack room if they choose.

Treats and mice!

We also have a very strict rule that all treats (even if it's still in an unopened bag) need to be put into a plastic container with a lid. If you have a barn then you will have mice and they will tear through anything including brand new treat bags that have never been opened. If you want your tack room to stay clean and nice then this practice is a necessity. Mice are very destructive and I have seen them tear up good riding pads just to make a nest.

If you have nice tack rooms and you get your boarders into the habit of keeping them clean, after a short while you won't need to worry about them anymore. Your boarders will value a clean tack room with everything in its place and nothing less will do.

Chapter 22

When a Horse Needs To Be Put Down

I knew the day would come when a horse needed to be put down at our farm but I had no idea of when it would happen. I had owned horses for much of my life and I had known friends that had to put their horse down and I must say it was heartbreaking. Now I was the barn owner and I knew it was going to happen and I was not sure what my responsibility was in all of it. I also didn't know how I was going to handle it.

I wanted to be there for my boarders if this day came for them but I didn't know how much I should comfort them or stand back and let them have their space. I was going to learn and I would come to realize that each time a horse passes on each owner will handle it completely different. Some will need a lot of help taking care of all the details and others will want to do it all on their own.

Many different reasons

I was about to see the world of horses and people like never before and in this case the very sad side of the horse world. Since we have opened our business we have put down seven horses over the years including one of my own and they all have been for completely different reasons.

I have experienced the pain and heartache that comes when you witness a horse break his leg and there is absolutely nothing anyone can do but watch and wait for the veterinarian to come. I have seen horses put down due to colic and blindness. I have watched horses put down because they were extremely old and it was time to say good-bye. I have seen horses put down because something neurological has happened to the horse and the vet knows the horse will not get any better. I have also seen the very sad side when an owner wants to put down a horse because of something extremely minor and was not life threatening at all.

Each time I have experienced the death of a horse at our barn it has been for a different reason. The other part of the situation that was new to me was how each person deals with having to put down a horse and the deep sorrow that goes with it.

How the owner of the horse deals with death and how the other people at the barn deal with it *when* it is not their horse can be very surprising to say the least. I have watched supportive boarders that come alongside the person that is hurting and comfort them and then I have witnessed the other side where people were angry in the barn because of what an owner was about to do to their horse.

As the barn owner I had to really dig deep and find out what my responsibility was and how I was supposed to handle an already emotional situation. I learned very fast that most people put in this situation need to know that what they are doing is the right thing and that they have support from the people around them.

Different opinions

Because you will have different opinions of when to put a horse down, you will have boarders that will put extra pressure on someone to keep a horse alive at all cost. Unfortunately in the real world most people don't have five or six thousand dollars just sitting in their bank account to cover a surgery or medications for their horse. During this time the best thing you can do as the barn owner is be supportive of the person that is going through this difficult time of making decisions regarding their horse.

I found it is very easy for people watching on the outside to judge and express what they would do but until you have walked in the shoes of someone that made that tough decision, you really don't have a clue. So as the barn owner you need to be there for your client during this difficult time. They are going to be looking to you for guidance, advice and reassurance.

You might even need to make it clear to the other boarders that you don't want to hear negative talk around the barn. You are going to be the one to keep the calm during the storm.

You are going to be the one to keep the calm during the storm.

Step up to the plate and be there for them

You could be asked to be there when the veterinarian comes to put the horse down. Some people cannot handle this and they will ask you if you would be there when the vet comes. I have always made it a priority to be there with the owners or without them if they choose to stay home.

The other part of your job will be to help make arrangements to dispose of the body if they ask. No one is ever prepared to say good-bye to their equine friend and when it happens your clients may not know who to call to dispose of the body or have the body cremated. You should keep those numbers on hand

and have them ready and in most cases your boarder will ask you to make the call and set up a time for pick-up because they will be too upset.

In all the years of boarding horses here at our farm, the owner of the horse has never been there when the truck has come to pick up the body. It is just too difficult and I completely understand this. I have always tried to have a horse put down in a place where there is not a lot of visibility from people or horses and we always keep a tarp on hand to cover the body after it is done.

The easier you can make this very difficult time for your clients the better. They need you and they won't realize it until it is happening. They will need you for comfort and guidance and leadership.

This will be the most important job you ever do on your farm so I encourage you to do it right the first time and you will never regret it. Your boarders will never forget either all that you did to make this extremely hard time bearable for them.

Chapter 23

The Challenges of Outdoor Board

The term "Rough Board" or what I prefer to call outdoor board will have a different meaning to many people depending on where they live. If you live in California or down south outdoor board is not rough at all but if you live in the Midwest or out East, outdoor board for horses can be pretty rough at times.

Growing up with horses in Southern California was a wonderful experience. We rode all year long and weather was never an issue. If the days were too hot we just didn't ride and they had the day off or we rode in the late evening when it cooled down. Experiencing Wisconsin winters and horse ownership was a new experience for me. Winters in the Midwest can be pretty brutal and if you own horses and they live outside in the elements it can be hard on them once in a while. There is a lot to watch out for to make sure they are staying healthy and keeping their weight up.

When we opened our barn we already had gone through a few years of taking care of my horses at our farm and dealing with the four seasons. Our horses were doing just fine and after all our new boarders came and the outdoor horses were settling in I really thought our outdoor boarded horses were going to be much easier to take care of than the horses that were stalled at night. After all there would be no stalls to clean or horses to walk out each morning and bring in each evening. I was in for a great learning experience.

Problems on the horizon

It was summer time when all our outdoor horses came and the job was easy. Fall arrived and the weather turned rainy and cold. We had built huge shelters that could easily hold three horses safely out of the bad weather and we put a cap on the number of horses that we would have in each paddock. Three was the magic number and it seemed to work. Isn't it funny how everything seems to work well when the weather is nice and the sun is out?

All of a sudden I had boarders that were calling concerned that their horse was wet or that the paddocks were too muddy. They were concerned about how much hay their horse was getting and the list started to grow fast. Because we were a brand new business with brand new clients, I was bending over backwards to make sure they were happy. I knew the horses were doing just fine but some of my new boarders were already struggling with their horses staying outside twenty-four hours a day and we hadn't even hit full winter yet.

Please bring my horse in

When winter was in full swing the days became very cold and we had some good size snow storms that first year and I had people calling me asking if their horses could be brought in for the night. Again, I knew the horses were doing great and their winter coats were long and heavy but I was starting to feel the pressure of these boarders to cave in and make them feel better.

We had stalls available in our smaller barn for the outdoor horses in case the weather turned terrible and the temperatures plummeted down to extreme negative temperatures. We also used them if they were predicting a huge snowstorm. Now I was getting requests to bring them in more often. I had not yet learned to be a barn manager and I was making the job much harder for my husband and me. We were bringing horses in all the time to please the boarders and with that came a ton of extra work and no extra money for the work. My new boarders were paying for outdoor board but they were getting stall board more often than was needed and at no extra cost to them.

I learned some very good lessons from those early years of boarding horses and dealing with outdoor boarded horses and their owners.

Harder on the owner than the horse

I realized that outdoor board is much harder on the owner than it is on the horse and in most cases the horses do just fine outside. It's the owner that struggles with most everything. I also learned that if you are not firm in how you are going to run your barn and outdoor boarding you will have a few clients that will push you as far as they can to get what they want. It can wear you down if you allow it and you will find yourself say "yes" to things that you will soon regret. I went through this during my first couple of years of running our business and it is not fun at all.

Hard to go back to the way it was

Once you give in to a request it is extremely hard to go back to how you had it before. If you bring the horses in when the temperature is ten degrees outside and you decide down the road that you won't bring them in unless it is minus ten degrees outside, there is a very good chance you are going to have upset boarders.

I believe now if you are very direct about how you run your outdoor board and are specific on how you handle weather and extreme temperatures, you will have very few problems. Your boarders will know what to expect and they will also sense that you are not going to change your mind for them.

I didn't know this in the beginning and I really didn't have a set of guidelines for outdoor board. I thought it was going to be so easy and it turned out to be very hard and frustrating those first few years. This is why I try to encourage anyone that wants to start their own horse boarding business to work as much as they can for a while with other barn owners and watch how they run their farm during all four seasons. It is truly the best classroom for learning to run a farm and dealing with horses, clients and outdoor board.

Challenges of Outdoor Board

Outdoor board has its own set of challenges and many of the problems that happen with outdoor board are due to owner error. Many people don't really understand how horses keep themselves warm in cold weather and they don't realize that some horses will stand out in the rain even if they are the only horse in a paddock and there is a shelter.

I have had boarders put show sheets on their horse to try to keep them clean outside because they didn't like the mud. This became an issue quickly because they were not water proof. I would come out in the morning and I would find the horse wet and shivering. I put a stop to that right away! I have also seen boarders come and pull blankets off their horse too early in the spring time and I have come out to feed in the morning and the horse is shivering to the point where I had to bring them into a stall and warm them up.

Part of your job is going to be educating your clients. Sometimes that's all they need. Once you talk with them and help them work through their anxieties then it will become easier.

When outdoor board is not a good fit

There are also going to be times when outdoor board is not a good fit for the horse or the owner and you will need to be honest with the owner when this happens. I have had this happen a couple times over the years and I had to talk with the owner and share what I was seeing and the struggle their horse was having. It doesn't happen a lot because I think for the most part horses will adapt as long as they have enough hay, water and shelter.

Remember, you will see their horse much more than the owner will and you will become very familiar with each horse's eating habits. Most people that board horses rarely see their horse during this time. They come out to ride and stay for an hour or two and when they are done the horse is put back out with their herd and off they go. They are trusting you to let them know if there is a problem.

One more thought-your idea of what bad weather is might be much different than your boarders. There will be times when you think the weather is fine and they will call wondering if you are going to bring the horses inside for the night. If you don't have an option to bring the horses in when the weather is extreme then your job will be easier because your clients already know there are no stalls available.

If you have stalls for use when a horse is hurt or sick then you might get a phone call now and then asking to use them if the weather is bad. You will need to be prepared for how you want to handle each request. It is part of having your own business and dealing with people. I want to assure you that the longer you run your barn, the easier it will become when it comes to outdoor board.

Feeding hay

Feeding hay and grain can have its stressful moments for sure. Most people believe outdoor boarded horses should be easier to care for because you don't have stalls to clean every day and you don't have to walk them out each morning and bring them in each afternoon. For the most part that is true but there are some challenges to feeding horses on outdoor board especially if you live in an area where the weather is a challenge itself.

I know every barn will feed hay differently and many people feed free choice hay in round bales or large square bales outside. They leave it out in the paddock and don't think about it until it is almost gone. If that works for you that is great but David and I prefer to feed twice a day at our farm.

I have found that if you have a few horses in a herd and they have to eat off the same bale there are many times when the low horse is going to struggle to get food if the more dominate horses don't let him eat. I have seen a few horses get beat up pretty good because they couldn't get to the hay. Another added problem is they lose weight. I believe it can be very stressful to the horse that is not getting enough food and it will affect the horse both mentally and physically. If you want to feed using a large bale of some sort then I encourage you to make your herd sizes a little smaller so that there is plenty of room for all the horses to eat.

We feed individual piles of hay twice a day and we feed enough piles for the number of horses that are in the paddocks. Some may say it is more work but I don't think so at all. We don't have problems with horses getting enough hay and they rotate from each pile and the stress level is pretty much gone. We also don't waste hay because they eat it all. When you use large bales or round bales there tends to be a lot of wasted hay and that becomes wasted money.

Picky eaters

If you have horses in your care that are picky eaters or just not good eaters, then this can become an issue once in a while in groups of horses that live together in outdoor board. If you are in the horse business long enough you will come across a horse or two that eats for a short time and then takes a rest. We have had a couple of horses at our barn that eat for a while then go off into the run-in to sleep and then they come back out later. Because they are in no hurry to eat, by the time they decide to eat most of the hay is gone and then a new problem arises. These horses become hard keepers and weight is always an issue because they don't eat very well to begin with.

I own a thoroughbred and even though she is in a stall every night, she is a hard keeper. She never finishes all her hay and many times she will eat for a while and then stop. I know that if I left her outside all the time she would be a rack of bones. It is just the way she is. Some horses are very nervous to begin with and they tend to eat and then walk around for a while to check out everything and then go back to eating. Many of these horses have a hard time keeping weight.

Remember that when you are boarding horses on outdoor board, you are going to get many different breeds and personalities. Most horses do just fine during feeding time but be prepared for that horse that comes to your barn and would rather take a siesta than eat at times. Those are the horses whose weight you need to watch closely. They are the ones that tend to lose weight overnight especially when it is cold in the winter

Most horses do just fine on outdoor board but if you are boarding horses and one of your client's horses is not getting enough food and is struggling to keep weight on it soon will become your problem. This is all part of your job as barn owner and barn manager and learning to work through some of these issues can be tough at times and it needs to be done with care. It might mean you need to help educate the owner about their horse and what you see going on in the herd and it might be something as simple as having a veterinarian out to check the teeth to make sure there is nothing going on in the horse's mouth.

I truly believe if you want to board horses then make it the safest and easiest environment for them at all times and they will be healthy and content and the owners will be very happy. You need to look at the big picture when you are running a boarding business and it will save you many headaches in the long run.

Feeding grain and supplements

Feeding grain and supplements on outdoor board has its own challenges. At my barn we only feed grain and supplements in the morning for our outdoor boarded horses. If I am going to be honest, it is a lot more work than feeding grain to a horse that is in a stall.

If you are going to feed grain then you need to decide if you are going to feed every horse out in the paddock or if you going to bring some horses into a stall each morning. The main problem will be how to keep the top horses from inhaling their grain and then going after the other horse's grain. It happens and you will find yourself becoming very frustrated if you don't have a plan.

Because our herds are very small I bring in a horse from each herd and feed them their grain in a stall. It is usually the horse that requires a lot of grain to begin with. Then I mix up all the grains and supplements and go out to the paddocks and feed the grains in individual rubber pans. It is pretty simple but works very well.

Once you know which horse is the top horse in the herd it is pretty easy to decide who to feed first and then go from there. Standing there waiting for them to finish is the hard part when you have other chores to do or if the weather is cold. This is why I only offer grain in the morning to our outdoor boarded horses. It actually takes up more of my time then feeding grain and supplements to twenty-seven stalled horses in our big barn.

Sorry but we don't do evening grain

We have had boarders that wanted me to feed grain at night (and they would pay me) but some jobs are not worth the money. I have always said no to evening grain and they find someone at the barn that can do it for them or they come out and feed it. It always works out. You will have to find out what works best for your outdoor board and then go from there.

Every boarding barn has its challenges and outdoor board is no exception. You will most likely go through a time of trial and error until you find what works well with your outdoor boarding business. You might need to modify things now and then and that is okay.

The best thing you can do is keep the communication open with your boarders especially if you see that something is not working and you need to make adjustments. Remember, your boarders are not at the barn when you are feeding and they have no idea what is going on so it is your responsibility to let them know if there is a problem.

If you communicate the concerns you have and then discuss with them the changes you will be making, the owners will handle it much better and they will respect you for taking the time to talk with them.

The bottom line

You have the awesome choice to design your outdoor board however you would like. There are many ways to run your outdoor boarding operation and you will find what works best for you but remember that however you choose to keep the horses in your care, it will affect the owners and it will affect how easy or hard your job will become. I am a firm believer in simple is better, long lasting and consistency always wins!

Simple is better, long lasting and consistency always wins!

Chapter 24

When Your Client and You Don't Agree

I never dreamed that I would be in a situation at my barn where a boarder and I didn't agree with how I ran the barn or took care of the horses. I really thought that taking care of horses was so easy and after all, how different could one person's idea be from mine? My learning curve was about to go way up.

Over the years I have met many people that own horses and for the most part we have a common bond. It is the love of the horse and we want the best care possible for our equine friends.

As our business opened and we were in full operation I spent the next year just getting used to all the new people and more importantly all the new horses. Things seemed to be going fine and then I put my first deworming note on the board. It was time to deworm all the horses on the property. I put out a reminder on the information boards in both barns and explained in detail the worming protocol.

My veterinarian told me...

After a day or so one of my boarders came up to me and told me that she was not going to do our deworming program. She had read somewhere that she should not use wormer on her horse and she also told me that she had talked with a veterinarian she knew and they told her not to use wormer at all. I am sure my face was blank as I was listening to her talk. I was not prepared for someone to come up to me and refuse to do something that was barn policy. On top of it this boarder had a strong personality and she actually intimidated me a little.

I told this woman that I would need to talk with my vet and get back to her on how I wanted to handle this. I went up to the house and sat there staring into space. I was not used to dealing with this kind of situation at all and now I needed to decide how I was going to handle it.

The next day I called my veterinarian and asked them about worming horses at boarding barns. After much talk and information to help me understand exactly how worming affects horses and especially the ones that live at a boarding barn I was ready to talk with this boarder.

I met with this person and explained to her that I had talked to my veterinarian and they had a completely different view of deworming and I explained the importance of worming your horse. This person became upset with me and started to argue and told me she was not going to do it! That is when I needed to make a decision quickly on how I was going to handle this.

I calmly told her that she would need to follow the protocol here at our barn and if she was not going to follow it then she would need to find a barn that better suited her. I didn't want to give her an ultimatum but I felt it was necessary in this situation and I was extremely nervous about how she was going to respond. This was not what I envisioned when it came to starting my horse business.

To my relief she backed down and said she would give the wormer. She wasn't happy and she did give it one time but soon she gave her notice and moved to a new barn.

I want my horse moved!

I have had a couple of situations where a boarder didn't like the herd that I put their horse in or wanted us to move their horse. I believed the herd situation was a good fit and for some reason they wanted their horse moved from the herd they were in.

Many times these issues are brought on by a horse coming in with a bite mark or possible kick mark. It can become very stressful because many times the boarder will not understand horse behavior and they don't know the difference between horseplay and horse aggression. They also don't understand that some horses tend to get in the middle of everything while others stay out of trouble.

I had one situation where a client became very upset because her horse had a bite mark on her side. Her horse never came in with marks at all and this mare was the top horse in her herd but this time she did and it was a good one. She right then and there told me she wanted her horse moved to a different herd. I tried to explain to her that I was not going to move her horse and then I talked with her about what was going on in the herd and the part her horse played in all of it.

She continued the next couple of weeks to ask me to move her horse and she became more and more assertive about it. I told her that I was not going to move her horse and that her horse was doing fine in the herd. This person stayed upset with me for quite a while but as time went on she started to see that her horse was doing well and she finally quit asking me to move her. She didn't completely agree with my decision but I believe she was willing to trust me and give it some time.

Coming to an agreement

If you are going to run a business then I can guarantee there will be times when you and a client will not see eye to eye. It is just the way it is and how people are. How you handle each situation will be completely up to you but you will need to decide if you are willing to let a client leave because they don't agree with something at your barn to the point where it is causing bigger problems.

You and your boarders will not agree on everything and if they had their horses at their own place there is a good chance they would do some things differently. That is fine but at your barn you need to know where to draw the line and when it can affect others at your place. In the situation with the worming issue, it could have potentially affected other horses and I was not willing to take that kind of chance with all the horses coming and going at our barn.

Remember, it is okay to disagree as long as it doesn't cause a health issue or safety issue at your barn. Your boarders need to know that you might be flexible to some degree but ultimately it is your decision as the barn owner about how things are going to be done.

Chapter 25

Handling a Boarders Difficult Horse

If you own a horse then you know at times they can be naughty and difficult. They have their good days and their bad days just like us. Many people search a long time to buy a horse and they may spend weeks or months looking for the perfect match for them. They get him home (or to a boarding stable) and it is a time for celebration. Everyone is over the moon at the beautiful new addition to the family and he seems perfect.

Sometimes after a few days or weeks bad behavior will start to creep in and everyone notices it but the owner of the horse. All of a sudden that horse becomes difficult to handle with some bad habits and now the perfect horse is not so perfect anymore. Many people will choose to get help to fix the issues their horse is having but there are some that will choose to ignore the bad behavior and make excuses for their horse. How do you handle these situations as the barn owner?

I have owned horses much of my life and I was used to handling my own horses. When they needed correction I gave it and it was over. I knew my horse's quirks and I knew when I could correct a problem myself and when I needed help from a trainer. I was about to learn that correcting your own horse is one thing but correcting a boarders horse is another.

Dealing with bad behaviors

We opened our boarding facility and in came the horses and people. We had many different breeds and personalities. Some of the horses were very quiet and some very excitable. As we got into the routine of hand walking each horse out each morning, I started to notice that some of the horses had bad vices and issues. Bringing the horses in at dinner time was even more difficult because they were anxious to get in the barn and the behaviors became much more challenging to say the least.

I have had horses bolt on me and get loose, try to bite me as I am walking them and make a dash through the gate and knock me over. I have horses that won't let you put a halter on very easily and in a few cases will take off as you are trying to put the halter on. Many horses don't know their space and they will push you over as you are walking them and many horses will drag you if you allow it.

David and I have been bitten, kicked, knocked over and dragged by difficult horses and in the beginning I wasn't quite sure how to approach the owner of the horse to discuss the serious issues we were dealing with.

Talking with the owner of the horse

There have been times over the years that I have talked with an owner and discussed the problems we were having with their horse and they were very open to correcting the issue. Then there have been a few times when I have talked with the owner of a difficult horse and they actually became upset with me and told me they have never seen the behavior I was talking about. At that point I knew they were in denial because the behavior was so bad that you could not miss it.

As the barn owner you are going to come across both types of owners and you are going to need to be ready to handle it. The first thing you need to realize is that no job is worth a preventable injury.

If you feel like you have a horse that is difficult to the point of being unsafe then you need to address it immediately. You might need to strongly encourage training for the horse and in the worst case you might need to put a time frame on it so that the owner becomes proactive on getting the bad behavior corrected. If you don't set a time limit on when training will start to correct the behavior, there is a very good chance that some clients will not do anything. I have seen that happen a few times at our barn.

You will run into the boarder that doesn't want to acknowledge there is problem and other times it is because they don't want to spend the money. If it comes down to the point where the owner is not going to get training for the horse then for the safety of everyone at your barn, you need to give them a thirty day notice. Remember, safety comes first!

The first thing you need to remember is no horse or job is worth getting hurt over!

Talk with the owner if there is an issue

Correcting a horse that is difficult can be hard at times if the owner is watching. There have been days when I am walking a horse back in from the barn and he is all over the place. If he starts to run me over I will back him up and make him listen and focus on me. I have done this while the owner is watching and I always wonder what they are thinking at that moment.

It is much easier to talk to the owner now because I have learned that it is not worth getting hurt, but years ago it was very difficult and I didn't want the owner to become upset. I don't worry about that anymore. Once you get run over a few times you will not feel bad about talking with the owner. It will make your job so much easier once you have a training plan in place to correct the issues.

Handling a boarder's difficult horse can be a delicate issue but if you handle yourself in a professional way and are sensitive in how you talk with your clients, the response is usually good. Remember that to many of your boarders their horse is like a child to them. It is hard for any parent to hear from the teacher that their child is misbehaving at school and the same will go for the owner and their horse. The big difference is that a horse weighs a thousand pounds and can hurt you in a second.

Sometimes all an owner needs is a little education and reassurance that if they get some training on the horse and follow through on their side when they handle the horse most of the issues soon disappear. You just need to make sure that everyone is on the same page when it comes to handling the horse.

The aggressive horse

Many years ago a horse came to our barn that was dangerous. I had never fully experienced what a dangerous horse would be like but now I had one at our barn. The horse was not only difficult but very aggressive towards people to the point where he would attack you if he could.

The owners were brand new horse people and knew absolutely nothing about horses. They bought this horse and three days later it came to our barn. As the horse walked off the trailer he was very quiet and I thought it was going to be an easy transition.

By the next morning I saw a completely different horse. He was tense and as you approached him his ears went back and his mouth opened wide with teeth showing. I had never seen such an angry horse except in pictures. I knew right away there was a serious problem with this horse and I suspected that the horse had been drugged by the previous owners. We couldn't get near the horse and when the owners came out that day, the mother went up to the horse and he actually opened his mouth and tried to bite her aggressively on her head.

The little girl became scared and after three days I told them that the horse was unsafe and dangerous and he needed to leave our farm. I explained to them about horse behavior and that this horse had some very serious issues that they were not equipped to handle and I didn't want to handle them either. I could not allow this horse to stay at our barn any longer.

These people agreed and the horse was shipped right back to where they bought him from. They didn't give up but looked around and ended up buying a very nice horse for their daughter and everything worked out much better.

Honesty is best but not fun at times

I hope you never have to deal with this situation at your barn but if you do, be honest with the owners and if they get upset and leave let them. If you have a horse that is dangerous, it is not worth the small amount of board you will receive each month to deal with it. An aggressive horse might change in the hands of a knowledgeable trainer that knows what they are doing but in the hands of most people a serious accident is waiting to happen.

The longer you handle other people's horses the easier it will become. You will know the horses behaviors better than the owners most of the time and if you need to address an issue with a difficult horse, you will learn the skill of communication under the most difficult and uncomfortable situations.

It is never fun to have to talk with your clients about their difficult or worse aggressive horse. Just keep in mind that these challenging times will help you become a stronger and more confident barn owner, manager and business person. Take each situation and learn from it and you will grow inside and out.

Chapter 26

When Things Get Broken, Who Pays?

If you have been around horses a long time then you already know that they are big, beautiful and they break things a lot. I had always boarded my horses when I was younger so I must admit I never paid attention to the damage that a horse did on the property. I never noticed how much the barn owner had to fix things that were broken. Now I get it!

David and I built our business from absolutely nothing but empty farmland. When we opened our business everything was brand new from the fencing to every stall in the barn. It was beautiful and we were so proud of it. I wanted it to stay that way.

As the horses came and time went by we really started to notice all the little things and sometimes big things that needed fixing. We had some stall kickers in our barn that would kick during feeding time and the stall boards were starting to take a beating. We had a few corner feeders that were kicked completely through. I even had a horse kick and damage a stall door. We have had two of our large outside water tanks kicked and broken. Those are just a few things to name but the list could go on and on.

What about when your clients break something? If you have people at your place then things will get broken sometimes. It is usually something easy to fix but none the less you are the one that needs to fix it. We have had many people break many different things through the years and most tell us but some do not. I can't tell you how many times David and I walk into the barn at closing time to find something broken and no one bothered to tell us. Be prepared if you are going to run a business because you will see it all.

When to charge the boarder for damages

Over the years I have had many barn owners ask me how I charge the boarders if their horse breaks something at our barn? Do I charge them right away or do I bill them when they move from our barn? Charging boarders for something that their horse has broken is not fun but a necessity for any business. The boarder is never happy about it and you might even get a person that wants proof that their horse has broken it. Some people handle it great and others vent as they are writing out the check.

I know of a couple of barns in our area that rent out their stalls just like an apartment. They charge a first month's fee and a last month's fee along with a "Repair" deposit. The repair deposit is really extra money to cover the cost of the things that need fixing after the horse leaves.

The barns that charge a repair deposit keep a log of items that were broken and then show it to the owner before they move the horse off the property. If you are good at writing down what needs fixing and keeping notes then this system might work for you.

I have always preferred to charge the boarder the repair fee as it happens. It is fresh in everyone's mind and usually they feel terrible that their horse broke something to begin with. I have found that if you wait too long and let too much time go by then people tend to forget and when you try to collect they might argue with you about it. I have heard of this happening to the point where the boarder becomes angry at the barn owner and ends up leaving very upset. If there was a good relationship before, it is now over due to conflict over damages.

I didn't want to deal with that kind of stress so I have always charged the boarder as it happens and we fix it right away and it is done. It has never caused a problem in business or personal relationships on our farm.

Okay, who did it?

There are going to be many times (more then you will be able to count) where things will get broken and you will never know which horse did it. None of them will fess up and they will all look at you with those big innocent eyes. It happens all the time when a fence gets pulled down. If you don't know which horse is the guilty one, there is not much you can do but fix it and eat the cost. That is part of having animals and I would encourage you to have a repair fund in place for those kinds of expenses.

If you have horses then things are going to get broken. When this happens you need to charge the boarder. Remember that they are going to feel awful about it when you tell them. If you do it with respect for them and kindness, the results will be much better. Put your client's feelings first and be professional at all times and you will have very little trouble being compensated for damages done by a horse.

One more thought-you want your place to last and stay nice a very long time. Your boarders will come and go and if you spend all of your own money fixing things that their horse broke it is going to cost you a lot and that is money that could be used for other improvements on your farm. You might even find yourself becoming bitter from it. Treat it like and business in all areas including repairs and you won't regret it.

Chapter 27

Are You Prepared For Special Requests?

If you are new to running an existing barn or are about to open a brand new facility, you might be in for a surprise when it comes to your clients and the requests you will receive. This part of barn management completely caught me off guard.

I had boarded my horses at a few different boarding facilities when I was younger and I think I was a pretty easy boarder. I didn't really ask for much except hay and plenty of it, clean water and shelter for my horse. I took care of most everything myself and if I needed help I usually asked another boarder if they could help me.

Many years later, I am now a barn owner and do not mind special requests as long as they are reasonable. It took me a long time to figure out what was reasonable and what would not work at our barn and now I am so much more prepared for special requests.

What is a reasonable request?

I have been asked to leave horses outside at night and bring them back in the barn each morning. I have been asked to put special lighting in a stall for the horse's coat. I have been asked to feed a certain type of hay and to wet the hay before it is fed. I have been asked to put the halter on a certain way and to make sure I take it off a certain way. I have actually been asked if I would allow a carpet in the stall of a boarder's horse! I have been asked to extend the hours of our barn and to make special exceptions for college students. I have even been asked to only allow certain disciplines to be in the arena during lesson times. The list could go on and on but I think you get the picture. Most of the requests I get are very reasonable but there have been some that were crazy!

Enough is enough

What I really want to talk about is if you are prepared for all the requests you will receive and how will you know when it is time to say enough is enough. Humans (including myself) will naturally want more if we are allowed. It is the way we are designed. If you don't set rules and guidelines on what is allowed at your barn, then before you know it you will have everything but the kitchen sink in your tack rooms and hanging in your stalls.

The only way to find out what requests you can and cannot honor is by experience and sometimes trial and error. Each barn is set up differently and depending on how your barn and turnout is designed will make a big difference on whether you can grant a request or not.

I have said yes to many requests over the years and realized later that it was not going to work. I have said yes to special lights in the stalls and found out later it wasn't going to work with how our stalls are designed and set up. Too many boarders didn't want lights shining in their horse's stalls and there was no way of changing it due to the grills that are between each stall.

We tried to do night turnout per a request and found out very fast that it didn't work at our barn and it made a ton of more work for David and me. It was not worth it so we quickly said no to night turnout.

When you change your mind

It makes it much more stressful to come back and tell a boarder that you have changed your mind especially after you already told them yes a day or two earlier. I have made that mistake a few times early on. If you find yourself in this situation you really need to do it with care and above all else be honest about why you can't honor the request anymore. Your clients will understand most of the time but be prepared because they will be disappointed. You can chalk it up to a great personal learning experience.

I have lost boarders because I changed my mind on a request and they decided to move their horse to a place that would allow what they wanted. It is part of the boarding world and you have to be okay with that and understand that it is part of having a business. You never know how a person is going to respond and you can't take it personally.

Every time you think you have been asked every request possible someone will come along and top it with a request you never dreamed of getting. One thing you need to remember is many of your clients came from other barns where things were allowed that you might not allow at your barn. It is an adjustment time for a new boarder and you need to be understanding about this.

One thing you need to remember is many of your clients came from other barns where things were allowed that you might not allow at your barn. It is an adjustment time for a new boarder and you need to be understanding about this.

The longer you run a barn, you will find that the special requests will become fewer and fewer. You will be established and people will already have a good idea of what you allow and don't allow. On the other hand if you are a brand new barn owner and your clients don't know you or how you do things, be prepared because it will be the sky's the limit when it comes to requests. Take it one request at a time and learn from each one what works and doesn't work.

One more word of advice-if someone asks you to put a carpet in their horse's stall, be prepared for an interesting relationship with that client. You just never know what you will be asked.

Chapter 28

Veterinarian's, Farriers and You the Barn Owner

If you have a horse then you will also have a veterinarian and farrier that you use. These professionals play an important role in the life and well-being of your horse. If you are in the horse industry then you already know this and I don't need tell you why they are important in the life of your horse. If you are running a barn the role of the veterinarian and farrier will become slightly different because they will become a very important part of helping you keep your business running smooth.

Your relationship with them will not just be about one horse any more. It will be about many horses and the entire barn as a whole. You will find out quickly that as much as you need them, they will also need you as the barn owner and manager. You will make their job easier in many ways and they will help make your job easier also.

Farriers

Most people that own a horse use a farrier. You will come across some people that choose to do their own trimming but not too many. Up until I opened my barn I only needed to worry about my horses and their feet. I had my farrier and never had any issues. I was about to have my eyes opened up to the many farriers out there and all the different beliefs about hooves, trimming and shoes.

I didn't realize that there would be so many different farriers coming to my barn after we were open for boarding and I was about to learn how complicated some people can make everything including trimming and shoes.

Five ways to trim a horse

After we were open for business we had about five or six different farriers coming to our barn. We had farriers that put on weighted shoes and farriers that only did a "natural trim." I was hearing about different ways of trimming and shoeing and each farrier had their own way of doing things. During all the years I boarded my own horses I never paid attention to different farriers at the boarding barns. Now that the farriers were all at my barn it was an eye-opener.

We have a lot of great farriers that come to our barn but I have also seen a few that I questioned their ability and training. I have seen farriers leave our barn and the horse was cut so short that he was lame. I have also seen a horse cut so short that he had blood coming from the bottom of his hoof!

You are going to see many things and as the barn owner you are going to be to the one to pick up the pieces if something goes terribly wrong. I have seen a few tears over the years because someone was trying to save money and hired a farrier that didn't know what he was doing and he ended up causing lameness in the horse that took months to heal. When this happens it is heartbreaking and it will become more work for you many times.

We don't have the problems with farriers we used to but we still have five or six farriers come to our barn and they are all different in how they handle the horse and even at times how they trim. If you find yourself in a situation where a farrier is causing hoof damage to a boarder's horse and it is clear that the owner doesn't know that the problem is from the trim, you might find yourself in a situation where you need to educate that person and advise them to get a second opinion. I have been in this situation a couple of times over the years where I persuaded the owner to get a second opinion about their horse's feet and the trim job.

Hopefully as a barn owner or manager you won't have any problems with farriers at your barn. If you are in the horse industry long enough you will see things that you have never heard of before. Be prepared for the farrier that really doesn't know what they are doing.

Above all else you need to remember that when something goes wrong even with a bad trim job, your clients will be looking to you for guidance and advice on how to correct the problem.

Your job will be to help them whether it means getting a second opinion from another farrier or in a worst case scenario you might even need to call the veterinarian. Sadly I have experienced both.

Veterinarians

We all need veterinarians for our horses and I am thankful every day for the great team of veterinarians we have come to our barn. My relationship with my veterinarians has changed a lot over the years and for many different reasons. I have learned that I need them and they also need the barn owners and managers for reasons much different than you would think.

Our barn is a forty horse boarding barn and with that many horses, it is only a matter of time that the vet is going to be called out to our barn for something. We always hope it is just for spring and fall shots but with horses anything can happen and many times they are called out for situations that need attention right away.

We have had to call the vet out early in the morning and late into the middle of the night. We have had them out for small lameness exams and for colic and even the saddest of situations when a horse needs to be put down.

Your relationship with the veterinarian

The relationship between you and the veterinarians that come to your barn is very important and for a few reasons. First of all, there are going to be times when you see that a horse is hurt and the vet needs to come out right away and the owner is out of town or you can't reach them. You are going to usually be the first one on the scene and the veterinarian and the owner are going to need to hear from you what is going on with the horse. Also, there are going to be times when the owner is too upset to handle the horse and they are going to need someone that is not so emotionally involved to help them especially if it is serious.

The veterinarian is not going to know the horse like you do as the barn owner and there is a good chance you will know the horse's behavior even better than the owner of the horse. You need to remember that not all horse owners come out on a daily basis to see their horse and some might only come out a couple of times a month. In these situations the veterinarian is going to depend on you to share with them any issues the horse might have with shots or being handled. As the barn owner or manager, your knowledge of the horse is vital in helping to keep the veterinarians safe under very stressful circumstances if they are unfamiliar with the horse.

As the barn owner or manager, your knowledge of the horse is vital in helping to keep the veterinarians safe under very stressful circumstances if they are unfamiliar with the horse.

Some horses will rear and lash out in panic at the sign of shots and it can put everyone in an unsafe situation. If you know that the horse has this tendency then sharing that with the vet is the best thing you can do.

Professional to professional

The relationship between you and the veterinarians that come to your barn will be a very important one for you as the barn owner. Your relationship will become equine professional to equine professional. I have had a few times over the years when I had a question or concern about a horse on our property and I would call my veterinarian and get their perspective.

The veterinarians need you and you need them and if you work to have a good professional relationship, it will make both your jobs much easier. When something comes up that is an emergency you will find out that you both will become a team.

Remember, you are not a doctor but your role is equally important. They don't know the horses on your farm as well as you do and together you both will become a perfect team to handle anything that happens at your barn.

Many barn owners don't see the importance of having a good working relationship with the veterinarians in their area and I believe they are losing out. If you are in the horse industry long enough it is only a matter of time before you are going to need them for something serious and you will be glad you have a respect and understanding for each other's roles.

Giving medications-Is it worth the risk?

Running a horse barn means you are going to come across many different kinds of medications. Many of them will become very familiar and will be used quite frequently and then you will see medications that you have never heard of before.

Along with running a horse business will come many different views about medications and what to use and how much to use it. Be prepared because you or your staff will be asked to administer medications and you will need to decide what you are willing to give and what you are going to say no to.

I never dreamed it would become so complicated when it came to boarders and medications but it did when we started our business and I was asked to do many things that I didn't agree with.

After about two years of running our barn I started to get a grasp on the world of medications and what I felt comfortable with. I have always had a lot of show horses here at our barn and when it is time for competition the pressure is high to make sure the horses are moving great and without any noticeable lameness or stiffness issues.

Learning about medications

During our early years I was asked to give certain medications for an extremely long period of time and of course I said yes at first. After a while I started to second guess my decision so I began to educate myself on the drugs I was giving and then I talked with my veterinarian. I found out some disturbing information about the drugs and the fact that I was giving them for a longer period of time than any doctor would administer them, made me very uncomfortable.

I stopped giving the drugs and talked with the owners of the horses. I told these clients that I would only give the medications if they could provide an approved prescription for the length of time I was to give the drugs. These people became very upset with me and said they didn't need a prescription and that is when I said I wouldn't give it anymore without doctor approval.

Eventually these boarders left our barn and my stress level went down a notch. I told myself that I would never put myself in this situation again and I never have.

Medications are common place

I am very aware that horses are given drugs all the time. What an owner does with their horse is their decision but if you are running a boarding facility and you are asked to administer a drug and something goes terribly wrong you are going to be responsible. I can guarantee that the owner will want to blame someone and it could be you.

Let me be very clear, it is not worth the risk! If you have written approval from a veterinarian then that is fine but if you are asked to give a medication for longer than the prescription calls for, you are going to have to make a decision. I encourage you to be very conservative on what medications you give without a written prescription from the vet.

I give medications all the time but I am very aware of what I am giving and I know I am not going beyond the limits of what should be administered. The best thing you can do if you have a question is to call your vet and talk with them and ask them about the drug.

The longer you are in the horse industry the more familiar you will become with the standard medications the veterinarians use in your area. If something new comes along from your client and there is no prescription with it then make a phone call first to make sure you are covered.

Please don't take chances with the horses in your care and don't take a chance with your business. You don't want to lose it all because you couldn't say no. It is never worth the risk.

When your boarder won't call the veterinarian

If you are in the business long enough you will come across a person that refuses to call a veterinarian when their horse is hurt. As the barn owner you will need to decide how you want to handle this situation if it happens to you.

There are a few reasons why an owner won't call a veterinarian when their horse is hurting but the most common reason is money. The reality is they don't want to spend the money or they just don't have it. I have had this issue come up at my barn a few times over the years and it almost never ends well.

As the barn owner you will need to be strong and firm if you feel a horse is in a situation where a veterinarian needs to come out and take a look. You might need to tell the owner of the horse that they don't have a choice. Each situation will be different and they need to be handled on an individual basis.

Remember that the bottom line is the care of the horse and if the owner won't do anything to help the horse then you will need to step in.

Check your boarding contract

I encourage you to make sure that your boarding contact contains a paragraph about veterinarian care and your rights as the barn owner to enforce veterinarian care. Also include that the barn owner has the right to call a veterinarian if the owner of the horse is not proactive in helping the animal. As with any contract, make sure you have your attorney look at your boarding contract and this area of veterinary care to make sure you are protected as the barn owner.

Chapter 29

What Do You Offer With "Full Service" Board?

Full Service board has a different meaning to many people. Whether you have a brand new business or have been running a horse barn for a long time, you will want to make sure you have a clear definition of what "Full Service" board is at your facility. Every barn offers different care and perks for their full service boarders.

Full service usually includes the feeding of hay, grain, supplement and keeping the water buckets clean and full. It also includes stall cleaning and turnout every day. When people ask me what we offer for full service at our barn, those services would be the base line to start. We do offer many other things as part of full service but in a client's mind these are the most obvious and of course important.

The not so obvious

Some of the not so obvious things we offer are inspections of each horse twice a day to make sure they do not have any cuts, abrasions, lameness issues or any other problems that might be going on. We will give medications twice a day (at no charge) and put fly masks on and take off on a daily basis. I will clean a cut and administer ointments on a wound if the owner can't make it out. There are many little things that as the barn owner, you will do for the care of a horse that your client will not see.

Full service in some barns will be much more involved. Some barns will bring the owner's horse in from the paddocks and brush them, pick their feet and have them tacked up ready to go when you pull up to the barn. Of course that full service comes with a price tag that is going to be much higher but some people want that option.

When you are talking with a person that is inquiring about your facility, be very clear about what you offer for full service board. I have had a couple of times over the years where a new person has come to board at our barn and there was some confusion on what we offer with full service after their horse was already moved to our barn. Things worked out but only after I explained in detail what we offer and don't offer at our barn. I now give out a sheet that explains all that we offer with our board and it is very detailed.

Your "Full Service" might change

As the barn owner, you have the wonderful opportunity to design your barn and what you offer. You may start out doing one thing but as the years go by you might change and modify what you offer for full service board. Our full service has changed over the years and we have taken away a couple of services that were included in the board early on but we have added several perks and other services as part of the board and it has worked much better for both my clients and myself.

I encourage you to take some tours of other barns and see what they offer for full service. It will open your eyes to what is out there and give you some new ideas. I still love to talk with other barn owners about how they run their barn and what they offer.

I have gotten some great ideas from other owners and used them at my barn. Be open to what is out there and it will only better your business.

Chapter 30

Are Your Boarding Rates Too Low?

Trying to figure out what to charge for horse boarding can be very challenging. I often talk with barn owners and many of them are not sure if they are charging enough or wonder if their board is too high.

How do you know what the sweet spot is for board and what your barn offers? I wish I could say it is an easy answer but it really depends on so many factors. Your location and barn amenities are two of the big ones that people look for in a boarding barn. Where you live in the country is another big one. What people look for in price and what you can afford to charge can be very similar or can easily be on opposite ends of the spectrum.

How much will people pay?

Where do you start and what are people willing to pay? When we were building our barn I asked myself these same questions. The first thing I did was a price comparison of all the boarding barns in my area that were similar in size. Then I looked at what they had to offer for hay and grain and amenities. I also looked at what services they provided for a fee and what they offered at no charge.

The biggest parts of the equation are your monthly expenses to keep the farm going. Your business mortgage and insurance are two big ones but depending on where you are located, hay will be your highest expense by far. Back then I was afraid to charge too much because we were a completely new business and I needed to make sure we could fill our stalls. I ended up charging less than my competitors which turned out to hurt me in the long run.

Don't go too low

As a new barn owner I was not confident enough in our facility and care to charge what I should have charged. I learned one major lesson from that decision: Once you set your price as a brand new business, you can't turn around a month later and raise the rates. You are stuck! Take your time and think it through before you advertise. I knew immediately that my rates were too low as the bills started coming in but it would be a year before I could raise them again. I learned a critical lesson about business just in this one experience of setting boarding rates.

One of the biggest reasons a person keeps their rates too low is because they are driven by fear. They are not confident in what they offer and the fear of losing clients overtakes them. Even if they have a waiting list or other barns in the area are much more expensive, they just can't take that step as a business person.

One of the biggest reasons a person keeps their rates too low is because they are driven by fear.

I always tell people that it does no one any good if you go out of business. If you offer a clean and safe barn with great care and wonderful amenities then people will pay for that. You need to remember that many potential boarders have already been to many other barns and they know what is out there. You are not surprising them with anything new. They know a good thing when they see it and they will pay a fair price to stay there even if it is higher than other barns in the area.

You need to remember that many potential boarders have already been to many other barns and they know what is out there. You are not surprising them with anything new. They know a good thing when they see it and they will pay a fair price to stay there even if it is higher than the other barns in the area.

Don't underestimate your value

One last thought-Once you open for business and you are working seven days a week, you will start to understand your value as the barn owner, barn manager, stall cleaner or the person who feeds and put the horses outside every morning and brings them back in every afternoon. You might be the one doing all those jobs or you might have employees but each job is vital to keeping the horses healthy and the farm running smoothly.

There is so much that your boarders will not see when it comes to the daily care of the horses and farm but those are the core elements of any horse farm. The people who do these jobs are the heart and soul and keep the farm running smooth. You can't do this job without them. Don't underestimate the value and worth of yourself or your employees and what you do for the care of the horses on your farm.

Chapter 31

The Issue Is Not Whether You Allow Back Shoes or Not

One of the most difficult parts of the job as barn owner or manager is dealing with the different views about horse care. It doesn't matter if your place is small or large, all it takes is two people and you will have differences of opinion. When we opened our boarding facility I was not prepared at all for the strong differences of opinion about horses and their care. I just assumed that everyone that came to board at our barn would have the same view or at least pretty close.

At our boarding facility we take care of forty horses that are many different breeds and sizes. We have many different riding disciplines which can make for a very fun and interesting barn. With all the diversity comes different ways of caring for each horse from feeding hay and grain to herd management. We had a situation come up years ago that tested my strength as a barn owner and leader.

Dealing with back shoes

We have always allowed horses to wear back shoes at our barn when they are outside in the herds. The only exception would be if the horse is an aggressive horse and aggressive kicker. If a horse has an aggressive personality and is a constant kicker then back shoes are not an option if he is going to be with other horses in a herd setting.

We had one client at our barn that had sold a horse and bought a different horse a week later. This person had owned a gelding and now had bought a mare and the mare was going to be in a different herd than her previous horse. The mare came to our barn and the transition went smoothly. We put her out with a small group of mares and the adjustment was easier than I anticipated.

After a few days this boarder came to me and told me that she noticed that one of the other mares had back shoes and this made her very uncomfortable. She wanted me to ask the owner of the other mare to remove the back shoes or to move her mare. I was in shock to say the least. This woman had been at our barn for a while and we never had any problems and now with her new horse she was worried about the back shoes on another horse.

I calmly explained to her that the mare with the shoes has always worn back shoes and she is a very quiet mare and doesn't have an aggressive bone in her body. I told her that it would be fine. The woman was upset but left for the day and I thought it was over.

The next day she came storming in our barn and started yelling at me about the care at my barn and was threatening to sue if her horse got hurt. I couldn't believe how upset she was. I knew I needed to stand my ground because I believed the herd arrangement for the mares was fine. I told her I was not going to change the mares or require that the back shoes be pulled off.

I stayed calm and I tried to turn the conversation into a positive resolution but that never happened. This woman was so upset and so worried at the same time about the back shoes on the other mare that she gave her thirty-day notice. I had to stick by my decision and not look back because I believed it was the right decision for this situation.

Stand behind your decision

Situations like this are going to come up in the horse world. You will find yourself involved in many discussions about things you allow and don't allow at your barn. At the end of the day it's not about whether you allow back shoes on a horse or not. It is about how you respond to the decisions you make regarding the horses in your care and if you are willing to stand behind them.

What you decide to allow at your barn is your choice and as the barn owner you have to live with the decisions you make. That includes the care of the horses in their stalls and out in the herds as well.

Some barns allow back shoes and some do not. Some barns mix mares with geldings and some do not. There are barns that allow kids to ride without helmets and then there are barns that do not. The list will go on and on. Once you make your decision of how you want your barn to run, stand confident in it.

Remember, it is okay if you have differences in opinion. Your barn will be the perfect place for many people and it is not worth the stress to change something because one person is upset. If you start doing that you will find yourself changing things all the time and it will make your job that much more difficult. Change can be good now and then but look at the big picture before you start making changes all the time.

Running a horse barn is a great job but learning to run it with confidence can take time and the tough situations that come up will be the best teaching moments of all. I have learned the most about barn management from those tough situations and now I look back and I am glad they happened because they helped me become a stronger, more confident barn owner. The same will happen for you.

Chapter 32

Do You Have High Turnover At Your Barn?

I have had the privilege of talking with many new business owners over the last year and many of them have only been in business for a couple of years. I listen to the problems and issues they are having and my mind goes back to when we first opened our boarding barn. I hear myself in every one of them and I can feel their pain and stress.

Starting a new business of any kind is extremely demanding and in most cases equine businesses have some degree of turnover in the first couple of years. This is hard on the business owner and it can be bad for business. If you can make it through those first few years and settle in to a nice routine then you are on your way to a successful horse business. The hard part is staying positive and finding out why you are having high turnover to begin with.

I thought they would stay forever!

When we first opened our boarding facility I was so excited about our new business and I thought it was going to be easy. I was prepared to work hard especially with forty horses to take care of. We were completely full when we opened and in my mind I believed that the horses that came that first month would stay for years. I give you permission to laugh right now if you would like. I truly had a lot to learn about people and owning a business.

Within our first year we had lost several boarders and we started to have many problems in the barn and they had nothing to do with the horses directly. I was learning very fast that I didn't know how to deal with the barn owner/client relationship. I had not defined my role or set boundaries and I was not leading the way a business owner needs to lead.

Things seemed great on the outside of our business but when I walked in the barn you could feel the tension and people were not happy. Because of my lack of decision-making or confidence in my decisions that I did make, it left many boarders unsure about the care of their horse. We also made many changes during those first couple of years because until you are in the mix of it, you don't realize what works and doesn't for your farm. The changes we made which were many in the beginning were very hard on my clients and I didn't realize that back then.

Identifying why your clients are leaving

Many barns struggle with high turnover and it is usually not one thing that sends a boarder packing. Identifying what the reasons are for high turnover can be difficult if you are the owner. It is very hard to see things clearly when you are in the middle of all of it.

Running a barn is a full time job and an exhausting job at times and when things are not going well it can be very difficult to fix the problems when you can't identify what they are. I believe this happens to many new business owners and sometimes it can be the turning point of whether a business grows or goes up for sale.

Back then I had no idea why our barn was losing so many boarders and why people were not happy. It took me many years to figure it out. Today our barn has extremely low turnover and usually the reason a person and horse leaves our barn is due to life changing events or the horse is sold. My clients stay and they are happy with how I run the barn. It has nothing to do with our indoor arena or the other amenities. Those things might bring them here to begin with but they stay for other reasons.

The relationship I have with my clients is built on trust and consistency and they know I will be looking out for their horse at all times. They are willing to ride out any changes I make because they trust me. Back when we opened our boarders didn't know me at all and I didn't know them. As a young boarding business we didn't have a history or reputation to live off of.

I now understand why they left

I now understand why many of our clients left in those early years. I had promised many things in the beginning and was not able to follow through with some of them. I was not leading and running the barn like I should have been. I was taking care of the horses but was having a difficult time making decisions and dealing with all the problems that our barn was having and it became out of control quickly.

The best way for any barn owner to really get a grasp of what is going on in their barn is to work it every day as the barn manager and that includes doing every other job on the farm. If you take the time to deal with the issues that come up at your barn and do all the chores for a while, it will open your eyes and you will understand your business inside and out.

Each experience will only help you grow with knowledge and confidence. Take the good days and enjoy them and take the bad days and learn from them. You need both to really learn and run a successful business. Eventually your good days will outnumber your bad days by many and you will remember why you wanted to start this business again. I sure did.

Take the good days and enjoy them and take the bad days and learn from them.

Honest feedback will help

If your business is young and your turnover is higher than it should be, don't panic. I encourage you to find someone who has been in the business longer (and has a positive and successful horse business) and who you trust to give you honest feedback. Share the issues you are having and take it one day at a time. Many of the problems will not be problems at all once you embrace your new title as business owner and run your barn with leadership.

Being a good leader doesn't mean, "My way or the highway." It means looking at the big picture and making changes with confidence and that can include making positive changes on behalf of a client's request. It might also mean making decisions that are not popular with everyone but that is okay and you need to stick by your decisions. You will never win a popularity contest when you are the barn owner and you need to be okay with that.

Remember, you are in a service oriented business and when you serve your clients and lead with confidence you will start to see wonderful changes happen in your horse barn and your clients will not want to leave. If your barn is having high turnover, look inside yourself first and see if you are doing everything you should be doing as the barn owner to run a healthy barn and business.

All new business owners go through trials and changes. How you choose to handle those situations will make the difference in whether your business will grow and become much easier to run or stay the way it is and just be mediocre. Don't miss the opportunity to really know what true success feels like when it is right within your grasp. Don't be discouraged. You can do it!

Chapter 33

Trainers at Your Barn

Let me start off this chapter by saying that I am not a horse trainer and have never been one. I believe it is one of the most difficult and dangerous jobs in the horse industry and the people who choose to become trainers are an amazing group of equine professionals. They not only work with large and unpredictable animals but they also have to work with or answer to the owners of those animals at the same time. It is a job that I believe takes a very special person.

I have seen many trainers come to our barn over the years and I must be honest and say that I have been shocked by many of the things I have witnessed through the years. As the barn owner I truly believe a trainer can help your business or hurt it terribly and you need to be very smart and aware of what they are doing at your barn. I have been on both sides and there is definitely an ugly side.

The power of a trainer

I didn't realize how much power a trainer can have at a barn until I became the barn owner. A trainer is able to provide something to a person that you as the barn owner cannot. The ability to ride a horse and live their dream is what every person wants and a trainer can help provide that.

The trainer/client relationship will become very strong and it will become greater than the barn owner/client relationship. You are giving their horse a place to live but the trainer is giving them wings to fly on the back of their horse. He is helping them achieve their dreams.

With that in mind if you and your trainer have a good working relationship and you both have the same ideas about horse care then they will be a huge asset for your barn. There is also the other side of the owner/trainer relationship. It is the side that can ruin a barn if allowed.

Doing things their own way

What if your trainer has his own way of doing things and different beliefs in how horses should be treated? What if your boarders start leaving because of your trainer's beliefs and practices? What if your trainer creates drama in the barn or is not doing the job your boarders pay him to do? What if your trainer is not respecting the rules you have set up in your barn and refuses to follow them in a passive aggressive way?

Let me tell you right now these things happen and they happen a lot. When we first opened our business we had several trainers come through our barn and they took over and the atmosphere became very negative and I started losing boarders. I was not strong enough to stand up as the barn owner and be very clear and direct about what I expected from the trainers that worked out of my barn.

The first thing you need to remember is that if you have several boarders that are upset or even worse leave, then I can guarantee that the trainer is not going to pay the income that you are losing. Can you afford the loss of income? The second very important point is, if you have a trainer at your barn and you are losing people because of what your trainer is doing then you might want to take a very long look at what is going on with your trainer.

It is fine if a client and trainer have a difference of opinion but if it starts to happen with several clients then there is a good chance the problem is with the trainer. Losing one boarder is not good but losing several boarders due to problems with a trainer in your barn is not acceptable at all.

The third point is that the trainers at your barn will never fully understand the pressure or stress that comes from running a barn and all that goes with it. They might have been barn managers but that is still much different than being the barn owner and dealing with the monthly bills and the responsibility that comes with caring for horses on a farm.

The empty stall

For many trainers it doesn't matter if a boarder leaves because it doesn't affect their bank account very much but you might be stuck with an empty stall and a lot less money coming in if you can't fill it right away. The trainer doesn't have the pressure to try and fill the stall unless they are renting it directly from the barn owner.

Many trainers drive in and give a few lessons then off to the next farm for more lessons. Their overhead is very low. The complete opposite happens for the barn owner. A boarder leaves because they are upset with the trainer at your barn and now you have an empty stall and every day that the stall is empty is another day of less income. That is just the reality of the life and business between a barn owner and the trainers that work out of the barn.

Understanding the trainer's world

The barn owner also does not understand all the pressure the trainer goes through at times either unless they are a trainer themselves. I have a wonderful trainer that works out of our barn full-time. She has been with us five years and I am amazed at what she can do with a horse. I will never fully understand her job and the pressure she feels with her clients and especially when a client is not happy. She will share her concerns with me but because I have never walked in her shoes I don't feel the same pressure she feels. It goes both ways.

The best thing you can do if you have a trainer that is working out of your barn is to sit down and talk with them about how you run your barn and explain your expectations and rules. They can also share what their training program looks like and how it will help your barn.

The relationship between the barn owner and the trainer is not just about the horses and clients. It is a working relationship that needs to have balance and a common belief in how a barn should run and strong agreement on how horses should be taken care of.

When it doesn't work

If your trainer can't follow your barn rules or believes he is above them then it won't work. If you believe that horses should be outside during the day and your trainer wants them living in a stall twenty-four hours a day then it is not going to work. If you don't believe in horses being tied up for hours on end or hobbling as part of training and your trainer does then it is not going to work. If you don't believe in aggressive bits and tack to force a horse to obey and move correctly and your trainer does, then it is not going to work!

I encourage you to think about all these things when you are interviewing trainers that might work out of your barn. Be honest and direct about your expectations and rules. At the end of the day you need to put your business first and if a trainer and you have a completely different view about too many issues regarding your barn then there is a good chance they will not be a good fit for your barn and business.

Once you go through a few trainers that have hurt your business you will appreciate and cherish the trainer that complements and becomes an asset to your barn. They are out there. You just need to be very deliberate in what you are looking for in a trainer to represent your barn. They will be part of your barn every day and many times the first person a possible new client will see when they come to your barn.

Be smart and don't be afraid to expect honesty and integrity from the trainers at your barn. Once you find a trainer that has the same value of life and care of the horses as you do then you will see wonderful things happen at your barn.

Chapter 34

Employees

When you can get to the point in your horse business where you are able to hire help every now and then or on a weekly basis, the feeling will be unbelievable. That is how it was for David and me.

When we started our business I didn't realize how financially strapped we would be and we would spend most of the next five years working seven days a week. Part of the reason we had so many money problems in the beginning was because of the poor decisions we had made in hiring a builder to build our barn. The results of those poor decisions led to lawyer fees and higher debt than we had ever dreamed.

Once we got to the point where we could hire help with the stall cleaning and Saturday morning chores, the pressure of working all the time lifted a little and the feeling was amazing. We started hiring people to come and clean stalls and with that came some new issues.

I was completely new to having someone work for me and I wasn't sure how firm I should be about the time it took to get the job done. I knew how long it took for David and me to clean all the stalls but we were also in a hurry to be done with the daily chores because there was so much more to do on the farm each day. The work didn't just stop because the stalls were cleaned for the day.

By the time Saturday morning rolled around I was over the moon with excitement to have other people come in and clean stalls. I knew it would only take them a few hours to clean all the stalls and it seemed pretty simple and straight forward. I never dreamed I would have issues with some people who came to clean stalls just one day a week.

Expectations for employees

What were my expectations for the people that would work at my barn? I really didn't have a clear vision of what my expectations were for my employees. In fact, I never gave it one thought until a few months went by and I starting losing money because we were paying out much more than we should have been. I was not direct in what was an appropriate time frame for a job to be finished and it was hurting our business financially. What should have only taken two hours to do was taking three hours or more and I didn't question it at the time. It started to affect us financially and we didn't have extra money to give out.

Even if you have employees working for you only one or two days a week it adds up quickly and when it is time to pay them, it will be a shock when it is more than what you had expected or budgeted for. That is what happened to us during those first few months.

I have come to learn that you need to be very direct with your employees about what you expect on the job and the time frame of how long it should take. They need to know that you have done this job many times over and you know exactly how long everything takes to finish the job. There should be no surprises.

Don't allow it to happen

I have talked to a few barn owners over the last year and one of the issues they are having is with their employees. They have employees that are coming in late and doing a poor job while they are there and taking twice as long to do the job as it should take. As the barn owner, if this keeps happening at your barn it is because you are allowing it to happen.

If you have employees that are coming to work late and doing a poor job while they are there, then you need to be the one to correct these problems. As the barn owner, if this keeps happening at your barn it is because you are allowing it to happen.

As the barn owner it is your responsibility to know how long a job should take. The only way for this to be possible is for you to live it and work it. If that means cleaning stalls then do it for a few days and see how long it takes. If it means feeding horses or topping off water buckets then do it. Farm duties are hands on jobs and even if your employees take a little longer or are slower than you would be, it should not be breaking the bank. I don't expect our employees to clean stalls on Saturdays as fast and David and I do them during the week. I expect them to be close in time but I also realize that because they don't do it on a daily basis it might take them a little longer.

Be clear about the time frame

The one thing I have done is to be very clear about the approximate time frame for each job on our farm. It lets the people who work for me know what I expect and what time they will approximately be done. This is a good system for any barn owner and employee and it is a very smart way to run this part of your business. Communication is vital when it comes to your employees and their job.

Work for board

Very few barn owners have excess money that they can waste and if you are not direct on how long a job should take, you might be losing money. As a boarding barn there will be times when you have boarders that will come and work for trade in board. It is very common for barns to do this but many times the compensation for the work done becomes a blur. The barn owner loses sight on how much he is paying out per hour and the boarder has no idea how much he is making per hour. Almost always it turns out to be a better deal for the boarder than the barn owner and this is a very easy way for a business to lose money fast.

The reality is your boarder might be getting free board for very few hours of work and if you add it up at an hourly rate you might be losing a lot of money each month. If you are on a financial shoestring already then you might want to think about an hourly rate instead and keep track of the hours that are worked by each person.

We tried exchanging board for help on the farm years ago with a boarder and before I knew it she had three horses and the lines were not clear on how much work she should be doing per horse or how many hours she was putting in each month and David and I were definitely losing money. It was a terrible way to run our business.

After that situation I went to an hourly rate and had everyone write the hours they work down on a calendar and then I pay them at the end of the month. It is very clean cut and there is no confusion. I treat it like a business and it runs like a business with employees.

There have been times when I needed to talk with an employee about their time and why it took so long to get a job done. It is not fun but I have learned it is part of the job. When someone new comes to work for me I tell them how long the job should take and if it runs over then they should see me first so we can see what the problem is.

The issues I had years ago pretty much don't exist anymore. I have wonderful people that work for us and they understand the job and they respect the fact that I don't have extra money just lying around to pay out.

Treat it like a real job

One of the biggest problems a barn will have with employees is that they don't treat it like a real job. The idea of working at a barn sounds so exciting and fun to most people. In the past I have had kids that come to work at our barn and all they want to do is play with the horses. They love the farm life but they don't realize how much work is involved and how physical the job is. Many of them quit after the first week.

Calling in and not showing up for work has been a problem in the past with employees and showing up on time was also an issue. Because David and I were running a business and had a time schedule to get the chores done it was extremely stressful when someone was late to work or just didn't show up.

I went through a time where the people that signed up to work just didn't show up. I finally had to be firm and let them know, if they were not able to come on time or were not going to show up consistently then they would not be able to work here at our barn. Some of them quit and it worked out because I was able to hire great people that wanted to come and do a good job and were very dependable. I have finally gotten to the point that if David and I want to leave for a couple of days with our family, we can with the confidence that the barn is in great care. When you reach that point it is a fantastic feeling.

Being dependable is a must!

If you are going to have employees then you need to make it very clear that you can't tolerate someone who is not dependable. The job of running a barn is already hard enough and if you have employees that don't show up you will be the one doing the work. That is how many barn owners burn themselves out. They don't have a good staff in place and they are stuck doing all the work when someone doesn't show up.

Working with animals is not the kind of job that you can close on Sundays and skip a day of work. The animals still need to be fed and watered and if you have an employee that doesn't understand this then you will need to find someone that will do a better job. They need to understand that it is a real job and that means showing up for work even when the weather is bad or it was a late night the evening before.

It is important to talk about what your expectations are and your business will run much smoother when it comes to employees. Remember, it is a business first and this is a very vital part of running any business.

Chapter 35

Happy To Say "Yes" But Learn To Say "No"

During the very early years of our business I had a very hard time saying no to anyone. I was so worried that if I said no, our boarders would get upset and they would leave. It was an incredible amount of pressure both ways. If they left I was worried that I would not be able to fill the stalls and if they stayed I ended up running around with all this extra work because I couldn't say no.

Those early years were exhausting because I was trying to work through all the kinks of a new business and I was making it much worse because I couldn't say no to my boarders at the time. I created so much more work for David in those early years and I didn't realize how much it was affecting both of us at the time.

It is okay to say *no*

It took me several years to learn that is was okay to say no and it wasn't the end of the world if someone left because I didn't give them what they requested. I think for women this can be an especially hard thing to do. In my thirties and forties I wanted to please everyone but I think sometimes as you get older it does become easier to say no and with running a business it becomes less emotional. At least it was for me.

I love nothing more than to tell a boarder that yes I can grant their request, but over the years there have been many times when I have said no and my clients have been just fine with it. Once you learn that it is okay to say no, it will be very liberating. It will lift a huge weight off your shoulders and you will enjoy your job so much more.

Be upfront with new clients

I have learned when a possible new boarder comes to our barn for a tour, that I am very upfront with them on what we offer and what we don't. I now will tell them right at the beginning if we can't offer what they are looking for in a boarding facility. If my barn won't work out for them, I try to recommend a place that is better suited for their needs. I think they respect the honesty and it is good for business.

I have talked to so many barn owners over the years that have boarders and have experienced the same situations. The people that have the hardest time with running their business are the people who still have not learned to say no when it needs to be said. It will eventually burn you out if you don't find a balance.

Just remember that for every time you tell a client no, you will have many more times where you will be able to tell a client yes! Don't let the fear of saying no stop you from running a healthy business. If you learn to say no, it will make each yes that much nicer.

Just remember that for every time you tell a client no, you will have many more times where you will be able to tell a client yes!

At the end of the day you need to do what is best for your business, family and yourself. Once you find a balance in running your business, you will be amazed at how much easier your life and job will be.

Don't try to do it all

We live in a world where people try to do it all and I believe many times it doesn't work out well. The stress of trying to do it all will eventually catch up with you. Remember that when you have a business in the horse industry, you are dealing with animals and your business will not close on the weekends or holidays. You will need to run your business differently than a business that is only open Monday through Friday. Someone will end up getting the short end of the stick and it will probably be you and your family. I had to learn this lesson very fast in our early years.

Today, I am always very happy to say yes, but I have learned to say no when I need to. This little concept has changed my life and it will change yours also.

Chapter 36

Do Your Boarders Understand the Barn Rules and Why You Have Them?

Can your barn have too many rules? I believe a better question is-Do your clients understand and know why you have the rules you have? I am going to venture out on a limb and say right now that many boarders do not understand why some of the rules are in place at most barns.

Let me share a few thoughts on why some boarders may not understand why you have the rules you have at your barn. First, it is not because your rules are hard to understand when you read them. I believe the reason many boarders don't understand the rules is because they have never lived on a working farm so in turn they don't have a full understanding of the daily work that happens on a horse farm. They may not understand how hard it is to keep everything clean when your floor and play area is dirt and mud.

Many of your boarders will be new horse owners and they do not have a true grasp of how accidents can happen very quickly on and off a horse and how safety is vitally important. If they have never watched an ambulance pull up to a barn because someone has fallen off and is badly hurt or been kicked by a horse and need medical attention, then they will not have a clue on how bad things can get.

Before you start pointing fingers I was that same kind of boarder years ago. I had boarded my horses at different places and I never once looked at all the work that was involved and when I was young I never looked at safety. The only work I did was brush my horse and ride. I threw caution to the wind as a teenager and thank goodness I never really experienced any serious injuries.

Barn rules are needed

Running a large boarding operation can get pretty crazy in a blink of an eye. I have always tried to keep our place running smoothly and efficiently but in order to do that I needed to have barn rules.

When we first opened we had very few rules only because at the time I couldn't really think of many. I thought to myself what could go wrong? I didn't want our place to be so strict that it wasn't fun for our clients. I again had a lot to learn about running a business and barn management. I was learning very fast that there is a fine line between having rules and being over the top with too many rules.

In our early years I would update our rules every year and I would add a few more. As each new situation came up, I would realize that I needed a rule for the problems that were happening in the barn and the list would increase. Now after many years of running our barn, the rules have stayed consistent for the most part. I rarely have to add a new rule only because as time goes by, you have a better understanding of which rules you need and which ones you don't. It just takes time and experience.

Take time to explain

If you are putting rules in place be open to explain why you have the rules you have. Barn rules are for keeping everyone safe and keeping your barn in order. Your clients may not understand the reason for some of them but if you take the time to explain, it usually makes things very clear and they will respect your rules.

I found out that I had boarders that liked the rules we had in place and then I had boarders that were irritated and even offended by all the rules. I have even had a couple people over the years that have moved to a different barn because they thought we had too many rules.

What some boarders didn't realize or understand is the fact that without the rules our barn would be a complete disaster and I was not willing to compromise on safety at all. A clean barn and a safe barn were two of the things that were very important to me and I believe vital to keeping a barn healthy and safe for both horses and people.

Clean up after yourself and your horse!

Another reason we put rules in place was for keeping the barn clean. Before we had rules about cleaning up, David and I would spend each evening picking up after our boarders and there was no reason for it. We had a problem with some people that didn't clean up after themselves and I needed to make changes in this area. I put rules in place and started to enforce them. It made a huge difference on the cleanliness of our barn.

I have learned after many years of running our barn that having rules is good for a barn and keeps everything running smoothly. Safety and becomes the driving force. I have lost boarders that wanted to board at a more casual (fewer rules) barn. I have also been fortunate to have wonderful boarders come to our barn that were leaving a barn with very few rules and the stress that goes with it. Those boarders greatly appreciated the rules we had at our barn because they had learned firsthand what a barn is like without rules.

Your boarders will come to love a clean barn and nothing less will do for them. It is easy to go from a dirty barn to a clean barn but it is very hard to leave a clean barn and go back to a dirty barn!

Your boarders will come to love a clean barn and nothing less will do for them. It is easy to go from a dirty barn to a clean barn but it is very hard to leave a clean barn and go back to a dirty barn!

Structure is not a bad thing

When your barn is small it is very easy to have fewer rules and keep things very simple. If you are running a large facility with many horses and people, you might want to think about a more structured barn. Remember structure is not a bad thing. In today's world we have lost some of the structure that is good for us. Let's face it, most of us don't like too many rules but they are a part of life and a horse barn is not an exception.

When you have your own facility and are doing the chores and cleaning up after people you will think twice about how you want to run your barn. When you have to call a parent because a child is hurt or worse call an ambulance, then you will think twice about having rules to hopefully avoid those situations.

Another part of the equation is the fact that your clients will forget from time to time about the rules. It happens at our barn and I find myself a couple of times a year sending out reminder notices. I have found as I get older that I have less patience and sometimes I need to write it down and read it over before I send out a reminder notice. Don't send out an email or letter when you are upset because it will only lead to stress between you and your clients. Take time to cool off before you send the reminder and make sure you are professional.

Reminders still need to be sent out but just remember that your anger is probably only towards one or two boarders that keep breaking the rules. Keep that in mind when you write your letter because you still have a lot of great clients that follow the rules each and every day.

I want to encourage you to end each reminder letter with something positive to say to your clients. It will set the tone and let the people who are following the rules know that they are doing a great job and it will put pressure on the ones that are breaking the rules to do better.

I have made the mistake over the years of becoming upset and saying things I end up regretting and then I feel terrible when the person I was talking to simply just forgot. Those are days I just want to crawl under a rock! We have been blessed to have fantastic boarders that really do take ownership of the barn and at times do a much better job of cleaning it than I do. I am forever grateful for those people who help keep it all running smoothly.

No surprises when it comes to barn rules

I believe the right boarders will come to your place and they will embrace how your run your barn. I encourage you to be upfront with future clients so they understand right from the start what your barn rules are and then there are no surprises. There are many boarding options available and you need to do what is best for your business.

You might go through many changes over the years but if you run your barn like a business it will run much smoother. Rules can be a good thing and yes a boarder might think you have too many rules. I don't believe a barn can have too many rules if they are common sense rules that keep everyone safe and help keep the barn clean.

Having rules and enforcing them can at times seem tiring and there will be days when you just want to let it slide and overlook something that needs to be addressed. It is part of any business owner's job. It will always be a balancing act but I truly believe the clients at your barn will love having a very clean barn with everything in its place. I would also venture to say that many of them will like that you have the rules you have. It almost sounds old-fashioned in today's world but a clean barn with rules is a nice barn to be part of!

It almost sounds old-fashioned in today's world but a clean barn with rules is a nice barn to be part of!

Your rules might change

One more thought-your core barn rules will always stay the same but some of your rules will change throughout the years. Our rules change a little every year as new things come up. Be ready to change your rules as your barn changes and grows because with new people, horses and riding disciplines will be different needs and new issues that need to be addressed.

If your barn is a hunter/jumper barn you will have rules that apply to jumping and all that goes with it. If you have a speed barn then you will address problems and create rules for safety when it comes to riding. If your barn is a multi-discipline barn then you might have barn rules for general activity and then you might have a separate set of rules for using the arena. As the barn owner you will set the rules for what works at your barn and you can change them as need be.

Vinland Stables Barn Rules

I have included what some of our barn rules and I will explain why we have them in place. Each barn will handle this a little differently but this will give you a starting point.

1. No smoking on the premises at all.

I think this rule is pretty clear but beware because if you don't have it as part of your barn rules, I can guarantee you will find cigarette butts on the ground and people smoking around the horses. We have "No smoking" signs in both our barns and this rule is posted and I have still found cigarette butts on the ground outside both barns a few times over the years.

2. No dogs allowed in the barns or riding arenas at all. You may bring your dog out to the farm and walk them but they need to stay on a leash.

Each horse farm will handle the dog situation differently. The first thing you will want to do is check with your insurance company to see what their guidelines are for dogs on a horse farm. We allow dogs but they must stay on a leash. The reason for this is the simple fact that most dogs are not used to being around horses and if they take off or see a cat and go after it, there is a very good chance they are going to run by someone that is riding and spook a horse.

3. Riders under the age of 18 must wear a helmet at all times when riding.

My farm insurance policy makes it mandatory that every person under the age of 18 needs to wear a helmet. You should check with your insurance and see what their guidelines are when it comes to helmets and riders. There are many barns that don't require anyone of any age to wear a helmet and it will definitely depend on your insurance and how your business is set up. Don't take the chance in this area. It is not worth the risk.

4. Correct footwear with a heel must be worn while riding. No sandals or tennis shoes at all while riding.

This is pretty straight forward and you wouldn't think you need to make it a rule, but if you don't put it in writing you will see people riding their horses in everything from sandals to high heels and flip flops! I have seen it all and there needs to be place where you draw a line and let your clients know what you feel is acceptable footwear.

5. No running or yelling in the barn areas, as this could spook a horse.

If you have kids at your barn you are going to have running and yelling. It is so much easier and safer to make it a rule and not have to worry about it.

6. Observe barn hours:
Winter hours: September 1st - May 31st 8am-8pm
Summer hours: June 1st - August 31st 8am-9pm

This is also very straight forward but so very important to have in your barn rules. Without barn hours written down in your rules, you will have people that will come out any time of the day or night.

7. All friends/visitors must sign a waiver release form prior to riding or handling a horse on the property.

If you are going to be running a horse business then you need to have liability waivers for all people who visit your farm and are going to ride or handle a horse. This is important and you need to make this very clear to your boarders. Any of their friends or family must sign a liability waiver before they ride. As the barn owner you want to make sure your business is covered in all situations. There will be times when you need to remind your clients about the importance of having the waivers signed.

8. Absolutely no riding in any stable aisle ways.

We have cement in all our aisle ways and it is not safe to ride a horse down them with cement, crossties and the congestion of people and horses everywhere, yet this has happened at our barn. You may not need this rule but if it has been a problem and you see it as a potential safety issue than make it a rule.

9. Never leave your horse unattended in the crossties. If you need to step away from your horse then please make sure someone is nearby to watch your horse.

If you have crossties I encourage you to have this rule. I have seen horses freak out in crossties and get tangled up or break them and it can happen in a second. Many people just assume that if their horse is in a crosstie that nothing is going to happen but many accidents occur in crossties and a horse can panic in a moment if something spooks them. I have also seen horses kick out at other horses as they are being walked by and I have been the recipient of a kick as I walked by a horse that was in a crosstie.

It is so much safer to make it a rule and always have someone by a horse that is in a crosstie. Even the quietest horses can panic if something frightens them.

10. Never tie your horse to stall grills at all. If you tie your horse to a stall grill and they pull and bend it, you will be responsible for paying for the repair and replacement of the damaged grill.

One of the things that drives me crazy is when you go to a barn whether it be for a horse show or clinic and you walk down the barn aisle and find bent grills on many of the stalls. It always reminds me of a crooked picture amongst a bunch of straight pictures. It looks terrible. That is how stalls begin to look when the grills are bent. One of the biggest reasons that stall grills become bent is because someone will tie their horse up to the grill and the horse spooks and pulls back.

If you are the owner of a barn and you want your barn to stay nice and look good for many years then you need this rule. If you don't put this rule in, you will have people tying their horses everywhere and your barn will start to show the damage. You need to look at the big picture and remember that your boarders will come and go but you will still be the owner until the day you decide you want to sell your barn and business. If you want it to hold its value then you need to make this a priority. If your stalls look terrible and are damaged it will lower the value of your barn.

11. If you get your horse from the paddocks or pasture make sure all gates are securely locked.

This is a no-brainer but it happens a lot more than you would think. You will find yourself reminding people every now and then about double checking to make sure the gates are securely locked. If you have never experienced a loose horse, you soon will once you start your own horse boarding business. Make this a rule and eventually it will become a habit for your boarders.

12. Clean up after your horse, BEFORE YOUR RIDE. This includes sweeping up the crosstie areas and placing the sweepings in the muck bucket. Clean up ALL manure in the arenas after use.

If you don't express what you expect at your barn, it won't happen. You need to be clear and direct and that includes keeping the barn clean. We make sure everyone sweeps up before they ride out of courtesy for the next person that wants to use the grooming stalls or crossties. No one wants to tie their horse up in an area that has dirt, hair and manure all over for you and their horse to step in. Also if you don't sweep it up, it will get dragged all over the barn and soon your barn will become a disaster. We have forty horses on our farm and all it takes is a few hours to make a huge mess.

If your boarders get into a habit of cleaning before they ride, before you know it they will like having a clean barn rather than a messy barn. It is a great habit to get into. I have never heard of anyone leaving a barn because it was too clean.

13. Adult supervision required for all young children at all times.

Your barn is not a gymnastics center or an ice-skating rink. It's not a pool or a park. It is a farm with very large animals that can spook and bite and kick. Accidents happen every day all over the world because someone left a child that was way too young alone with some horses. All it takes is a second for something to go wrong and as the barn owner it is not your responsibility to watch children. You need to make the age of child supervision very clear.

You are going to come in contact with many different types of parents and some of them will hover over their child until they are eighteen and then you will find some parents that will turn their child loose with a horse as young as eight or nine without any parent supervision. It will be your job to set the guidelines for your barn. It is much better to be conservative on this subject or you may come to regret it.

Remember, your barn is not a babysitting business and very young children should not be left alone anywhere on the farm otherwise you might find them climbing in the hay loft and cutting open hay bales for fun. I can say this from experience!

14. When you worm your horse please make sure to clean up any droppings of wormer that may fall to the floor. It is toxic to dogs. If your horse is not behaved when it comes to worming then please administer the wormer in their stall.

The reason I included this in our barn rules was because I was finding wormer everywhere. I always knew when someone wormed their horse because half of it would drop to the floor and they would not clean it up. I included the part about wormer being toxic to dogs because if you allow dogs in your barn and they eat some of the wormer it will make them very sick. Even if you don't allow dogs in your barn, it is a good practice to get into.

15. Do not put your horse in another horse's stall without the owner's consent. If your horse messes in the stall or drinks the water, clean the stall and fill up the water bucket. Leave the stall better than you found it.

You might find this rule odd or wonder why I have it at my barn but it was added several years ago. I had a problem with trainers and people using stalls that were not their horse's stall because it was in a convenient location for them. They would put the horse they were riding in a stall close to where they were working because they didn't want to walk down to the other end of the barn to use their own stall.

I didn't realize this was happening as much as it was until I started to get complaints from the people whose stalls were being used and not cleaned afterward. I put an end to this practice immediately.

16. During the spring when your horse is shedding or if you are clipping your horse, please put all hair in designated garbage cans by grain room or grooming stalls. If you only have a small amount of hair it can be put in the muck bucket. Do not use trash cans in tack rooms or lounge at all.

We made it a rule that horse hair needed to be put in designated garbage cans because I was finding tons of hair in the lounge trash cans and in the tack room garbage cans. First of all, horse hair will attract mice and is perfect for them to build a nest with and it also smells. Our tack rooms started to smell bad and soon I was finding horse hair and baby mice in many places.

Horse hair is beautiful on horses but not floating around in the air or in a mouse nest. You need to be very direct when telling your boarders where to dispose of any kind of garbage and horse hair.

17. Clean the wash stall immediately after you are finished using it. Be sure to sweep up all debris and put into muck bucket to prevent clogged drains. You also need to empty the drain of all hair and mud. If any water gets out into the aisle, take a broom and brush it back towards the drain. Please double check to make sure the water is turned off after use.

If you have a wash stall then you are going to want a rule about the proper care and cleanup of your wash stall. If you don't tell your boarders what you expect, your wash stall will become a disaster after a few uses. To avoid plumbing problems with the drain you are going to need to be very clear on how to clean the drain and that you expect it to be done after each use.

If you start this practice right from the start it will become a habit and a great habit for your clients to get into. I didn't have this rule when we first opened because I never gave it any thought. After a couple of months and a plugged up drain (with water everywhere) I learned real fast that cleanup needed to be done after each horse was bathed. A large amount of dirt and hair comes off a horse and it will plug up any drain pretty quickly if not cleaned out on a regular basis.

18. When bringing your horse into the barn from the paddocks please stay on the path at all times. If you walk your horse on the grass when the ground is soft or wet, it will tear it up.

This rule is in place because we live in Wisconsin and we get a lot of rain. Our farm is in a low lying area and our ground is very soft much of year. If we had our farm on high ground this most likely would not be an issue. I do have places that our boarders can hand graze their horse but if I let them walk their horse anywhere on our property our grass would become a mess especially in the spring and fall.

Many of you will not need this rule at all but if you tend to have a lot of rain and you are in a low lying area like we are, you might want to think about this one. You want your facility to look nice and that includes the grass area. It is good for business when your farm is kept nice and well maintained and the grass is part of that picture your clients and the public will see when they drive into your farm.

19. Turn off the lights if you are the last one to leave the barn. Helping to conserve the electricity will help keep the fees down.

This is a pretty straightforward rule but you need to have it. I wish I could tell you that the lights will always be turned off but that is simply not the case. There are going to be many times that you will find a light left on. When people are not paying the bill they just don't think about it. This rule is a nice reminder. You will want to also have signs posted in certain areas to help remind people to turn off the lights.

Adjusting to your rules

As you can see from reading my barn rules they are pretty simple. This was just a sample of what your barn rules might look like. Every barn is going to be different and you will change your rules many times throughout the years as you find out what needs to be addressed. Even though you have barn rules, your boarders will need reminding from time to time. That is just the nature of the business and people.

One more thought-remember many of your boarders will have boarded at other barns before they come to your place. That means they will be used to a set of different rules. Give them time to adjust and become familiar with the way your barn does things. You might need to explain why you have some of the rules you have and that is fine. Take the time to answer their questions so they have a clear understanding. It will start things off right for them and you and it won't be a guessing game.

Riding arenas and rules

If you are running a boarding facility and have riding arenas then you are going to want arena rules in place. It is a must for safety. Many of your boarders will not know proper arena etiquette and for many of them it might be the very first time ever using an arena. They may not be aware of how an accident between two riders can happen in a moment's time so it is your responsibility as the barn owner or manager to educate them.

Having a written list of arena rules is something I pass out to every new boarder that comes through our doors. Arena rules will be different depending on the disciplines at your barn but the core rules should be similar.

Here is a sample of our arena rules for Vinland Stables.

Vinland Stables Arena Etiquette and Rules for Safe Riding

1. When entering the arena be sure to announce your entrance WELL BEFORE you enter the arena. Call out, "Coming in" or "Door" and listen for a reply that it is okay to enter. Riders inside arena will either say "OK" or "Stop, wait a minute." Remember, they don't know you are entering the arena and they might be riding by at the same time that you want to enter.

This is the most important rule we have for our indoor arena. Many people that come to our barn do not know to stop and call out before entering an indoor arena. They don't realize that a horse could be moving by at any time. We had a horse spook because someone came walking right in without stopping and the little girl that was riding fell off and broke her arm. This is the first arena rule I mention to all new people at our barn.

2. Lunging horses-There are only two horses allowed to be lunged at the same time in the arena. If you come in and two horses are already being lunged, you will need to wait until one is done. Please be aware of where you are lunging your horse. If other people are already riding or having a lesson and you come in, please ask them, "Where would be a good area to lunge my horse?" When horses are being lunged they take up a lot of area with the lunge line and it makes it very hard for people to ride around them. Please just communicate with each other.

When you have horses being lunged and horses being ridden together in an arena, it can become a safety hazard very quickly if it becomes too crowded. We have a very large 80 x 200 indoor arena but once you put a couple of horses on lunge lines in there it quickly becomes very tight to ride around.

I have this rule because I have seen three people try to lunge their horse in our arena while others are riding. Some of your boarders are not going to know what can go wrong and they will only be thinking about their horse. You have to bring it to their attention.

3. The *Inside* of the arena is toward the center. The *Outside* is by the wall.

This may seem like common sense to many of you reading this, but you will come across many riders that do not know these simple terms. It is better to put it in your arena rules then to have confusion later.

4. When passing another rider from behind, always pass on the inside (not between the rider and the wall). When meeting another rider coming toward you, pass so your LEFT shoulders meet. Clockwise rider goes inside; counter clockwise rider goes outside by wall.

There is a good chance this will be confusing to some of your clients the first time they read it. The best thing to do if your client doesn't quite understand is to give them a visual. That always works much better.

5. Please call out your direction of travel if you will be traveling across the diagonal of the arena or need to do lateral exercises on the wall or the diagonal of arena. Please be courteous and understand when directions are called out, it is temporary and that the rider would appreciate you to free up the requested area for the moment.

This is another rule that you will need to explain and possibly give a visual for your clients that are not familiar with these terms.

6. Stop your horse and stand still whenever a rider is having trouble controlling their horse.

This is a good practice for everyone to get into and most boarders understand this already.

7. Do not stop in the line of travel of another rider. If you need to stop/dismount, please do so in the center or corner of arena.

I put this in as a reminder to my clients so they become aware of where they are dismounting. Many times a rider is so focused that they forget there are other people riding in the arena.

8. If you are coming into the arena and someone is having a lesson, please be courteous and stay out of the area that they are having a lesson. If the rider is using up a good part of the arena, then communicate with the trainer and find out where the best area would be to ride.

Communication is key when it comes to trainers and lessons. We have a trainer that gives lessons all day long and we don't have any problems because everyone makes a great effort to communicate with each other. Once you can get your boarders and trainers to start communicating, most of your arena issues will disappear.

9. Please be sure to talk to each other. We are all equal in this arena and are all here to help one another. The best thing to do if you are unsure about something is to ask.

This last rule is pretty self-explanatory. Communicate, communicate, communicate!

As I said earlier you will come across many clients that have never ridden in an arena before. Take the time to educate them at the beginning and answer their questions. I will have something new come up that I haven't dealt with before and when that happens, I usually will tell the person involved to give me a little time and think about the situation before I decide how I want to deal with it.

Even after all these years I still get hit with new issues every once in a while. Thank goodness the issues are small and usually easy to resolve. Remember, the longer you are running your barn and that includes everything that goes on in your arena, the easier it will become to problem solve. The experience you will get running your barn every day will be the best teacher of all.

Chapter 37

Is Your Barn Set Up To Handle The Special Needs Horse?

We have been blessed over the years to have so many wonderful horses stay at our facility. We have had horses as young as four months old all the way through thirty-four years old. Each horse holds a special place in my heart and each one came with their own quirks and vices. Most of the horses in our care have been very easy to take care of but we have also had a few horses come here that had special needs.

As a very new barn owner, I was not at all prepared for the horse with special needs. I never even gave it a thought. To show you how naive I was, I just assumed all the horses would live in the paddocks we designated for them and that was all there was to it. I give you permission to laugh right now if you want. I am laughing as I am writing this because I really had a lot to learn about horse management and especially the horse with special needs.

The senior horse

If you are in this business long enough you will eventually come across someone that wants to bring a very senior horse to live at your barn. Are you ready to take on a senior horse and do you have accommodations for a horse that might need to be living with only one or two other horses?

We were not set up for this early on and our first senior horse came to stay at our barn shortly after we opened our doors. He was a magnificent old Warmblood that had truly lived an amazing life. He had a wonderful show career and for years after was a faithful school master to many riders. His owner lovingly retired him and now he was going to live out the rest of his days enjoying life.

When he came to our barn we put him in with a herd of geldings and he was doing okay but it really was not an ideal living situation for him. He didn't want to deal with the antics of the young geldings and after a while he seemed to become stressed. After much talk with the owner we decided to create a new outdoor paddock just for him and one other horse. It would be our "Senior Paddock" and only used for the horse with special needs or the senior horse that needs some quiet in his life.

That was one of the best decisions we have ever made at our farm. Since we have opened there has always been a horse or two that uses this senior paddock. I truly believe it has been healthier for the senior horses in our care and it gives the owner piece of mind. They don't have to worry about their horse at all.

The different challenges

Over the years we have had horses with many special needs. We have had to soak the hay and grain for a few senior horses that had difficulty eating or digestive problems. We have had horses with moon blindness that needed special lighting in their stall at night. We had a couple of horses over the years with Navicular. If it's in a stage which makes it painful and difficult for the horse to walk, then special arrangements should be made for turnout. Even some horses coming off the show circuit will have their own set of special needs if they are not used to going outside and being with other horses. There can be an adjustment period for some of these horses and they need to be handled with care and patience while they take time to adjust to their new life.

Deciding if you can care for the special needs horse

I encourage you to take a look at your business and see if you are ready to handle the horse with special needs. You should decide if you want to take on a special needs horse or the horse that has special dietary needs before they come to your place.

You will come across many different needs of the horses in your barn and you should have a good understanding of what that horse requires for his care and a good idea if you can provide that care or not. It is so much better to be honest with the owner if you can't provide the proper care needed in certain circumstances.

Please don't try and fit the special needs horse into your way of doing things. That usually doesn't work. You need to be able modify your way of doing things to accommodate these types of horses for it to be a success for you and the horse in your care. If you are not able to modify your program for the horse with special needs, then it is far better to be honest and let the client know before they move the horse to your farm.

Don't try to fit the special needs horse into your way of doing things. That usually doesn't work. You need to be able to modify your way of doing things to accommodate these types of horses for it to be a success for you and the horses in your care.

The last years can be the best years

One more thought-Some of the warmest and best memories I have of the horses on our farm have been from the horses that needed special care. They have warmed my heart in a special way and I feel so honored to have been given the opportunity to care for these great animals that lived a long rich life.

If you choose to care for the senior horse or horse with special needs at your farm you will find a joy that runs deep and you will see what caring for these horses with a servant's heart is truly all about. It will take you to a much deeper level of love and respect for these magnificent horses that we have the honor of taking care of.

Remember, they do whatever we ask of them for so many years of their life. Let's do what we can for them when the time has come for them to retire and relax and enjoy their life. They deserve it from us.

I encourage you to talk with others in the boarding business if you are just starting out to find out how they handle horses with special needs. The more you educate and prepare yourself to handle these horses that come to live at your barn the easier the transition will be for them. For many of them it will be the last place they live. Wouldn't it be great if their last years were their best years at your farm?

Chapter 38

When a Horse Doesn't Fit the Program That You Offer

I never thought we would have a situation where a horse wasn't adjusting well to the living arrangement we have here at our farm. There have been a couple times in the last ten years where a new horse has come here to board at our barn and the horse struggled to relax and fit in. Both those times involved our outdoor boarded horses. Outdoor board great for most horses but once in a while you come across a horse that would rather be in a stall especially at night.

One of the common mistakes a brand new horse owner will do is buy a horse, maybe a Thoroughbred or a show horse that has lived his entire life in a stall and decide they want to put them on outside board immediately-No adjustment period of any kind and no thought about the breed and dealing with the weather. In many cases the transition can make the horse even more stressed and the owner will not understand why this is happening.

Difficult time adjusting

As the barn owner it is your job to inform your boarder if you see that a horse is having a difficult time adjusting to the living arrangements at your barn. They are paying you and entrusting you with the care of their horse and if you see that a certain arrangement is not working for a horse in your care then you need to let the owner know.

It is not easy to tell a client that they need to think about stall board if the outdoor board is not working for their horse and the same would be true for the other way around. There are horses out there that become stressed when left in a stall. They may eventually settle down but there are times when outdoor board is a better suited living arrangement for some horses.

When a change needs to be made

If you are boarding horses you will eventually run into a horse or two that has a hard time adjusting and there might even come a time when changes need to be made that the owner of the horse will not be happy about.

I had to talk with a boarder one time about a horse that was on outdoor board and I felt after a couple of months that this particular horse was not adjusting well at all. The horse was losing weight because he was hardly eating and pacing a lot. This can be normal behavior for a horse that has just been moved but if it last a couple of months then there are bigger issues. I suggested to the owner that they should wait for a stall opening and I believed that the horse would settle down if he could be in a stall at night.

They took my advice and when a stall opened up we moved their horse to the big barn and he went outside during the day and came in to his stall every evening. After about a week his personality started to change and he became calmer and seemed much happier and content. He didn't have to deal with the bad weather anymore and he started to eat more and put on weight. This was a situation where the horse benefited from the changes made to his living arrangement.

You need to be prepared because once in a while you will get a horse that is having a difficult time and the owner doesn't believe what you are telling them. They don't want to make the changes you are suggesting and you might even get to a place where you need to talk with them about what is best for the horse and not give them an option.

No more options

Years ago we had a situation where we had a horse come to our barn that had never been in a stall and the adjustment was hard. The horse was used to being outside every day and the owner wanted to keep him in all the time for showing. This boarder only wanted the horse outside for about an hour each day.

The horse started to have a meltdown on a daily basis and tore apart the stall and the rubber mats on the ground. We kept waiting for the horse to settle down but he never did. I finally had to tell the owner that the horse needed to go outside during the day with all the other horses. If she wanted him to be in a stall all the time she would need to find a barn that was better suited for her and what she wanted to do. I explained to her that this was not healthy for this horse and it was causing a lot more work for David and me because he was destroying his stall. She decided to move her horse to a different barn that was better suited for her and it was better for all of us.

I hope this situation never happens to you but if you are boarding horses then you will meet many people from all walks of life and they will have many different ideas about horses and living arrangements. There is a good chance their ideas will be a little different than yours and you will need to be ready to have an educated response when they start to question how you do things at your barn.

Not every horse or person is a good fit

As the barn owner or manager you never want a boarder to leave because what you offer is not working for their horse. But the reality is not every horse or person will be a good fit for your program. If you have tried everything you can and it still doesn't work then it is better to suggest to them to find a barn that better fits their needs.

There are plenty of barns that board horses and each one has something different to offer. You will have new clients that come to your barn and they will share with you all the issues they were having at their previous place and how it affected their horse. Many times once they are at your barn you will see a completely different horse than what they described.

For the most part most horses do just fine after a slow adjustment with good care and patience. Keep your eyes open for red flags and keep the communication open with the owner. If you are a multi-discipline barn then some of the issues you might have will only appear because some breeds need to be handled a little differently when it comes to the daily care and feeding program.

Remember that a Thoroughbred is not going to handle the cold Midwest winters on outside board as well as a draft horse. Think of those kinds of things when you are talking to perspective clients and don't forget to ask what breed of horse they have. It might make a difference on where you put them at your barn and it might reduce any possible stress in the future.

Chapter 39

You Can't Always Perceive How Your Clients Are Going To See Things

Owning and running a horse boarding operation was something that I never dreamed I would do in life. I had been around horses most of my life but my professional life was always in the school system in one form or another. When I made the change to taking care of horses and doing chores every day it was a much bigger change then I expected.

Handling horses every day is a great job and there are days when the horses are well behaved and then there are days when I have to be firm with some of them. The one thing I love about horses is that they are pretty easy to read. They let you know when something is wrong and it is immediate. They really are the easiest part of the job.

Becoming the barn owner and barn manager put me in unfamiliar territory. I had never been in a leadership position before and learning to run a barn and trying to make my boarders happy was tough at times. Those early years were difficult because I was not leading and in retrospect I was too worried about pleasing everyone. I now know that is impossible but I still try to make it a great place for our clients and their horses.

Over the years many people have walked through our barn doors and I have had the privilege of meeting so many wonderful people. If I am going to be totally honest I have also had a few people leave here because they didn't like the way we ran our barn. That can be very hard to take especially when you are trying your hardest each and every day to do what is right.

The reason a boarder leaves your facility will be for many different things. Some of them will be good reasons and some of them will shock you. Learning to act professional at all times is important and I have blown it a few times.

The longer you are in this business you will learn to have a thicker skin and as long as you know that you did the best possible job anyone can do, you can't control how your client perceives it.

Finding a mentor is a great thing

If you decide you are going to work in the horse industry and you are going to be working with clients I encourage you to find a mentor who can guide you and help you through the difficult times. Many jobs have mentors to help young leaders in a management position but I have not found that in the horse industry especially in the boarding world.

It really is so much healthier for a person to have a sounding board and to be able to talk with someone when you are dealing with an upset client, past or present. When looking for someone to mentor you find someone that has been in the business awhile. A great mentor is someone that will give you honest feedback and who you can be totally honest with. You might not like how honest they are but if they are there to help you with your business and make it all that it can be, then honesty is something that is vital for growth for anyone.

Remember, you can't control how others are going to react to you as the barn owner or manager and once you put yourself in the leadership position, there are going to be many times when you will not be popular for the decisions you need to make at your barn. Learning to handle each situation with calmness and integrity takes time and experience. Don't be too hard on yourself. A great mentor will share with you some of their mistakes through the years and how they learned from them.

Make a list

Take time each day to have a few quiet moments and think about your goals for your barn and what kind of atmosphere you want to have. I encourage you to make a list of your goals on one page and your struggles on another page. Keeping track with a list will help you stay focused on yourself and your goals. It will be a good reminder of how you would like to change in certain areas of your life and how you run your business.

Making a positive effort to work through the problems that will come up and learning from each one will mold you into a stronger barn manager and a more confident person. Also, for me prayer is a big part of all of it.

One more important thought-If someone from the past comes back to share the things that upset them years before, let it go. You will never be able to read people's minds and if they don't share with you during the time that they boarded with you don't let it ruin your day because they have come back many years later to complain. It is not worth it. Let it go and take the upper road. Be professional and move forward. If you know in your heart that you did the best job you could do, then be happy with that and keep doing what you love to do.

Chapter 40

Is Your Chore Routine Stressing Out the Horses In Your Care?

Having a routine seems like a foreign idea these days. We live in a fast paced world where people are in a hurry and the routine of our life gets pushed aside on many levels. When this happens I believe it can creep into your business life and your barn. Then add the horses in your care into the equation and it can make for stress on the farm at times. Having the routine of *no routine* can really be stressful on a horse.

Even though our world has become busy and crazy at times, the horse and his world have not changed. His life is simple and he just wants a few consistent things. He wants to feel safe, have food, water and shelter from the weather. Now I know that feeding time is not going to be exactly the same down to the minute each morning and afternoon but at our barn try to keep it as consistent as possible. I truly believe that if the horse knows what to expect each and every day then they handle things much better.

If you run a boarding facility you are going to deal with horses that are very easy going and never get bothered by the feeding schedule and then you will have horses that come unglued when the routine has changed.

They are no different than us in many ways. Some of us do fine with living on the edge and never worry about what is next and some of us do so much better with a routine in our life. Now as humans we have the upper hand and we can think things through rationally and not panic but horses were created differently and for them it is about survival. They are not going to think things out rationally all the time and it would be wrong of us to expect them to.

Creating a routine

I really believe that if you create an atmosphere at your barn where your chore routine is pretty consistent you will find out that you will have fewer problems and the horses will be much calmer. Now I am not talking about when you are on the road for a horse show or trail ride. They need to learn to be calm under those situations also, but if their home is a place where consistency with food and daily care are pretty much the same seven days a week then when they are asked to go to a show or trail ride, I believe many times it will spill over and they will handle the outside world much better also.

If they are constantly stressed at home because the chore routine is very sporadic and inconsistent then there is a very good chance some horses will carry that over with them to the horse show and on a trail ride. I know it depends on the horse but why even take a chance when there is no reason to.

Some horses handle inconsistency better than others and you will find your job so much harder if you are rushing around because you are feeding a couple hours later than normal. This is so true for both morning and evening chores.

Take a closer look

I encourage you to take a look at how chores are done at your farm and if you notice your horses acting like they might be stressed then take a closer look at the routine at your farm. All it might take is some simple adjustments to create an atmosphere that is calming for the horses in your care.

Remember that setting a schedule for your barn is an individual decision. We feed our horses very early in the morning but if you want to feed at a later time and they learn that routine that is fine. Just be consistent with whatever time you choose and you will have happier horses.

Consistency is a win/win for the horse and the owner. There is nothing better for your barn then happy horses and happy boarders!

Consistency also affects your clients

Also one more important thought-Everything you do as the barn owner will affect your clients also. I have talked with many people over the years who were frustrated because the barn that they kept their horse at was not consistent and when they came out to ride their horse in the morning, they never knew if their horse was going to be fed or not when they got there.

That can be very frustrating for the boarder as well as everyone else involved. If your clients know what your feeding schedule is and know that it doesn't change then they can work around it if they want their horse to have some food before they ride. Something as simple as consistency shows your boarders you care about the horses. Consistency is a win/win for the horse and the owner. There is nothing better for your barn then happy horses and happy boarders!

Chapter 41

Blanketing and How It Affects Your Job

Growing up in Southern California with horses is much different than having them in the Midwest. The number one reason would be the weather. In Southern California the weather is warm and hot. That pretty much sums it up most of the year. Once I moved to Wisconsin, I was about to learn what having four seasons was truly all about. Adjusting to the winter time is one thing but having horses and dealing with the four seasons is a whole different world.

I had never blanketed my horses out in California so I was going to learn about blanketing very quickly and my first job in Wisconsin was twenty five years ago and it was at a show barn. Every horse was blanketed most of the year except during the summer and many of them went outside for only a short time. The barn was very consistent about how they viewed blanketing and for the most part it was pretty simple. I was learning a lot about blanketing in all four season and it was easy to see how it could become very complicated very quickly if allowed.

Fast forward and we opened our boarding barn. Our business opened in the summer time and as each horse came to our barn everything went pretty smoothly. The weather was beautiful and the horses were outside every day. No blankets were seen until fall came. Then my job as a barn owner was about to become more complicated than I anticipated. As the blankets went on, my job became busier and even stressful at times.

Many different ways of blanketing

I had boarders that came with as many as five different blankets for all types of weather and the temperatures played a big part in all of it. I had people that double blanketed and then I had people that changed the blankets according to the temperatures. I had people that wanted a full face cover on their horse and many wore neck covers. Some would put sheets on that weren't water proof which caused problems and I even had one person who put a full face show sheet on and that was a disaster when the horse went outside in the wet and mud. I have had people try to use cool down sheets as blankets for outside which doesn't work either.

Too hot or shivering

I have had to talk with boarders that had too heavy of a blanket on their horse in the spring and the horse was sweating and even foaming a little because they were way too hot. I have also seen the other end of it where I have had people pull their blankets off too early in the season and then we get a cold snap and the horse is shivering outside. Both scenarios are upsetting and as the barn owner I had to go into unfamiliar territory and talk with the owners each time something like this happened.

Why did I let any of this bother me? There is a very good answer. Because as the barn owner/manager, when something doesn't fit the horse properly or is not waterproof you will be the one that sees the horse when they are wet and shivering or sweating and full of foam underneath the blanket. You will be the one to see bad rub marks where the hair is missing and the blanket is so tight that it looks like it is choking the horse.

As the barn owner you will see how stressed the horse is when they are shivering or sweating. The reason I let this bother me is because I love animals and it is very upsetting when I see a horse struggle and suffer because of the mistakes and choices their owners make.

As the barn owner you might think it doesn't concern you but if you care about horses then it will. I was never able to ignore what I saw because I could see how uncomfortable the horse was. I have come out to the barn and found a horse tangled in his blanket and you could tell he had struggled during the night. His straps were tangled up and he was not able to get his leg completely through the straps after he got up from lying down. I have come out to the barn in the early morning and found blankets completely off a horse because they had broken straps and the owner didn't want to spend the money to fix the blanket. When I think about what a horse goes through when the blanket is halfway off always upsets me because you know he probably struggled to get to that point.

What many people don't realize is that all it takes is a horse to panic in his stall while he is tangled up in his blanket and it could result in a terrible injury. We had one pony that boarded at our barn that became lame for a while due to a blanket that he was entangled in and in the process he must have panicked. His recovery was about two weeks.

The full face cover

I had one boarder that was persistent on having a complete face cover on his horse but the problem was it didn't fit well and the opening for the eyes kept moving. I would tell him that it was a problem and needed to be addressed and he kept telling me it fit just fine.

Then one day his horse was outside in the paddock with five other geldings and they were pulling on his face cover and his eyes were completely covered because the openings for the eyes had shifted. My husband noticed it and right away ran out there and pulled the face cover off. That was it. I told this person that we were not going to allow face covers at our barn anymore. I didn't feel it was safe to have a horse in with other horses with a full face cover on because they will pull on it with their teeth and it is truly an accident waiting to happen.

Finding what works and doesn't work

Through many trials and errors I have finally learned what works and doesn't work at our boarding facility. I am very particular that the blanket needs to fit correctly and all the straps need to be in good working order. If a strap is broken then they need to fix it as soon as possible. I don't allow any kind of sleazy (whether full body or head and neck cover) to be put on for outside. If they put on any type of show sheet it must be water proof. I have brought in too many cold and shivering horses in our early years that were wet due to the rain and they couldn't dry out because the sheet they had on wasn't water proof.

Depending on where you live will make a huge difference in blanketing. Obviously if you live in a hot state blankets will not be used most of the time. But if you live in the Midwest or out East, the weather can really cause some horses to struggle if they don't have the correct blankets on for the season, temperatures and weather.

Everything your clients do

As the barn owner everything your clients do will affect you and it could make your job harder at times if they do some of the things that I described earlier. Not all your clients will do these things but if you are in the horse industry long enough, you will eventually see some of it at one time or another. If it's at someone else's barn that is one thing but if it's at your barn, it will become your problem if you care about the horses that are living at your farm.

I now spend time trying to educate new horse owners on what type of blankets to buy for each season and temperature. I like to keep things very simple myself with my horses and I try to pass that on if I have a client that wants to know how I do things when it comes to blanketing.

I am not telling you all these stories to scare you at all. I want to educate you on some of the things you will see once you start running a barn and then you can decide how you want to handle these issues. It will seem uncomfortable at first but if you talk with your clients and explain what can happen and how to find the right fitting blanket they will appreciate it and you will have fewer problems in the long run.

Charging a fee for blanketing

One more bit of advice-If you are going to offer blanketing as a service at your barn then it can add a lot of time to your already busy day especially if you have a lot of horses that need blanketing. I encourage you to treat it as a separate expense and charge your clients for this service. I have seen barns include blanketing as part of the board fee and that is fine as long as you have it figured into your monthly board rate so you are not working for free. Blanketing is very time-consuming and you should be paid for this added service.

If you don't get compensated for your time you will soon regret it after you have been putting on and taking off blankets for a month or so. It will get old real fast especially when they are very muddy and dirty. It is just something to think about. Remember, you are running a business and your time is valuable.

When horses destroy each other's blankets, who is to blame?

Blankets and horses are quite the combination. We go out and buy these beautiful blankets in many different colors and styles and they look so nice the first time we put them on our horse. They are bright and clean and our horse looks like he just came out of a Dover magazine. I must admit I love buying new horse blankets.

The next day we come out to the barn and drive into the driveway and look across the field and see our horse with what used to be a bright, new blanket barely hanging on him! As we walk out to get him we can tell that something is hanging down one side of him but we are not quite sure what it is. Then we discover that our new blanket is torn down one side and part of the outer shell is hanging almost to the ground. If you have horses, (especially geldings) there is a very good chance you have experienced this.

Who did it!

It is upsetting for anyone and the next question is who did it? As the barn owner, without a doubt you will see this happen at your barn a few times during your career and the geldings always seem to be the guilty ones!

Every year by the middle of winter, we have blankets that have small and large tears in them and you will find duct tape on a few of them trying to hold the tear together. I have also mended my torn blankets many times trying to get another year out of them.

As the barn owner you want to decide how you are going to handle the client that wants to put the blame on another horse for their torn blanket. Believe or not, just this one issue can cause problems between boarders. I have had a few boarders over the years that wanted their horses moved to new paddocks because their horses were playing and coming in with many new tears in the blankets.

After a few years of running my barn, I decided that I was not going to move a horse because they were playing with another horse and their blanket was torn. If I did that for one boarder then I would need to do it for all of them and I would be moving horses every day and my life and job would become much more difficult.

I want to be compensated!

What do you do when a boarder wants to be compensated for a torn blanket? I had a situation come up where a boarder came to me and wanted to be compensated for the torn blanket on her horse. She wanted the owner of the other horse to pay. I was not prepared for this and I had to choose my words wisely. I did explain to this woman that no one is responsible for what happens to blankets out in a herd setting and that we need to remember they are horses and this is part of how they communicate and play. Very gently but firmly I told her she needed to accept this otherwise she could pay for private turnout. In this situation she handled it very well and this experience helped me grow as a barn manager.

Educating your boarders on brands of blankets

I realized early on what particular brands of blankets held up to playful geldings and moody mares and which ones did not. I started to educate my boarders on the difference in a poor quality blanket vs. a high quality blanket that will stand the test of playful geldings. If a person owned a horse that played a lot and was constantly coming in with a torn blanket then I suggested a brand that I have seen work well over the years. I think now after ten years, I could be a sales rep for a horse blanket company!

As the years went on in my boarding business I found myself educating many of my boarders about horse behavior and how it all connects together. Even something as simple as blanketing a horse can become complicated until you understand what is happening out in the herd. Then it usually becomes pretty clear and it is easy to fix.

If you are the recipient of a playful horse that likes to come in with a new tear on his blanket, then I suggest for you to try a better brand. If you are the barn owner that has clients who are upset because their blankets are torn, then it will be your job to encourage them to buy a better made blanket that will stand the test of almost any horse.

The bottom line is that your clients are going to have to understand that this is part of having horses and they cannot try to blame other horses and they can't expect the owner of the guilty horse to pay for the damaged blanket.

If a client has willingly agreed to have his horse out with other horses, then these are some of the chances you take when they are in a herd setting. Your client may not like it at the time but they will either except it or pay for private turnout.

Most of the time after a few torn blankets, your clients will buy a much better and tougher brand to use and most of the issues with torn blankets will disappear.

Who ever thought that there would be so much to talk about when it comes to blanketing and barn management!

Chapter 42

Herd Management

Herd management will be one of the most important parts of your job as a barn owner and barn manager. If you are going to run a barn where the horses are turned out every day then you better have a good grasp on what herd management is all about. Every decision you make with the horses at your farm will be noticed by every one of your clients and if there is a problem in a herd, they will be the first to let you know.

When we started our business we had almost forty horses show up at our farm within a month's time. It was absolutely crazy to say the least. I had all these new horses and I didn't know their personalities or their owners and it became stressful pretty fast.

I thought I knew herd management but you really don't know it until you have to put a bunch of horses together in small herds and hope they get along. Looking back, that first month was a complete blur. I don't think I have ever been so tired and trying to find a good fit for each horse we boarded proved to be very challenging.

Do they know their horse's personality?

When you are in charge of the horses in your care one of the best resources you can use to find out about a horse's personality is the owner of the horse. The big problem with this idea is the fact that about ninety percent of all horse owners really don't know what their horse is like in a herd setting. They don't know if their horse is typically a dominate horse in a herd or at the very bottom. During that first month we even had brand new horse owners come to our barn with zero horse knowledge and they didn't know anything about the horse they had just purchased. I was pretty much starting from ground zero with all these horses.

The other part of the situation I was dealing with that first month was the fact that many of the boarders didn't know the difference between horses playing and horses fighting. That is something that has not changed over the years and many people still don't know how to recognize the difference in the two behaviors.

Their hurting each other!

If you are going to be dealing with herds and herd management then you are also going to be educating your boarders when a situation arises. There are going to be times that you will get a call that two horses are being aggressive towards each other and your client is going to want you to do something right at that moment.

There have been times when a boarder had driven into our farm and caught the tail end of what looked like fighting or aggressive behavior and right away my phone will ring. It can make people very nervous when they see horses playing or becoming aggressive and if their horse is in that particular herd it will bother them much more.

Denial and the horse owner

I have had a couple of boarders over the years that owned horses that were dominant and aggressive but in the owners mind their horse was the one being picked on. It has caused stress between me and the client because when I would try to explain what was going on in the herd with their horse, they didn't want to hear it.

In one situation I lost a boarder and horse because I refused to move their horse to a different herd. The herd that their horse was in was the best one suited for him but he was also a horse that looked for trouble and he had a streak of getting himself hurt. It became very stressful between this client and me and they ended up moving to another barn. I tried reassuring this person that the horse was doing fine but there was no changing her mind and in the end it was better for all involved when she moved.

Take time to watch the horses

I always encourage our boarders to take time during the day and come out to the farm and just watch the horses. If they would take the time to watch their behavior, it would teach them more than any book could and it would teach them a lot about their own horse's personality.

You will come across many people that want to learn and will try to come and watch the horses in a setting that lets them be horses, but many people work and are busy during the day and would rather just come out after their horse is brought in to ride.

You will need to find a balance between all the different clients you have and how they view horses and herd behavior. Ultimately as the barn owner you will have the final decision on where a horse is going to be placed and you will need to stand strong with your decision.

Ultimately as the barn owner you will have the final decision on where a horse is going to be placed and you will need to stand strong with your decision.

We are friends so our horses must be friends

I have run into a few people over the years that were friends and would trail ride together so when they moved to our barn they felt their horses should be in the same paddock together. The problem came in when I told them that the horses would be in separate paddocks because it would be a better fit for both horses. I explained to them that even though they would trail ride together, it doesn't always mean their horses are going to get along when left alone in a herd setting.

As the barn owner you will not always be able to put horses where your clients would like them and you need to be okay with that. If you try to place a horse wherever the client would like the horse to be, you are in for more work than you dreamed. Your clients will not know the other horses in the herd and their personalities and if you are persuaded to give in against your better judgment you might really regret it.

As you can see herd management is so much more than dealing with horses. You are also dealing with the owners and it can become complicated if you allow it. This is where you need to be a confident leader and make decisions on the herds and not look back. If you start giving in to requests to move a horse here and move a horse there, you will be causing so much more work for yourself and if will burn you out.

You need to remember that every time you move a horse, it takes them time to adjust and the first couple of days are spent figuring out where they are in the herd. Every horse goes through adjustments and it happens every time they are moved. You also increase the chances of a horse getting a kick, bite mark or hurt every time a horse is placed in a new herd. It's all part of how they communicate and once they settle down things usually go pretty well.

Really get to know them

You will have horses with many different personalities on your farm and after a while you will know them better than the owners when it comes to their eating habits and how they behave in the herd setting. If you watch them long enough they are so predictable and as horses leave your barn and new ones come in, it will become much easier to place a horse in a herd because you will already know the established horses and herds quite well.

Herd management is ever changing and even the weather and seasons can cause a change in a horse's personality at times. It will also be a balancing act between you and your clients and you will learn when it is time to be firm and stand your ground on your decisions and when it is time to move a horse because it is not a good fit at all.

You will have many trials and errors in herd management and you will grow more than you ever expected in knowledge of horse behavior. You will find out what works and doesn't work at your farm. You have the greatest classroom right in front of you so take the time and seize the opportunity each day to learn from the horses in your care and watch your knowledge of herd management grow to new levels. It is truly amazing to watch these beautiful animals each and every day.

Chapter 43

Mixed Herds or Not?

If you ask ten people if mares and geldings should live together there is a good chance you will get ten different answers. One of the most often asked questions I get from potential boarders looking at our facility is do we separate the geldings from the mares? Most of them are fine with my answer but there have been a few people that didn't agree.

At our boarding facility I do have a couple of mixed herds and it works well but it is not by chance. I really need to know the horses I am putting together and if a gelding in any way acts "Studdish" then he is not in with any mares ever on our farm. It works the other way also. If a mare acts "Marish" all the time and has a hard time being around geldings then I need to find a paddock with all mares for her. I have seen the personality of a very quiet gelding change fast because he was put in with a mare. There is always the element of surprise with horses but I try to keep those surprises very few and far between.

As the barn manager you are going to really need to learn how to read the horses in your care and if you are going to combine geldings and mares then you will need to know what to look for if problems start to occur.

We have a couple geldings on our farm that can never be with any of the mares because of their behavior. I don't make it a habit to combine mares and geldings but we have two paddocks that are combined and it works well only because both the mares and geldings are very calm and their personalities do not change when they are with each other.

A bad experience with mixed herds

One of the biggest hurdles you will come across as the barn manager is earning the trust of a new boarder that has come from a very bad experience dealing with their horse and mixed herds. There is a chance that they were at a place that didn't know how to group the horses and their horse got the brunt of it.

I have heard of barn owners putting horses together in herds and under no circumstances are they willing to change the horses even if problems arise. It could be that they don't know what to look for or that they don't have enough paddocks to be flexible. They might even believe that the horses need to work it out no matter what. Either way, when a client comes to your farm that has gone through a bad experience they are going to be bringing with them the fear that it will happen again.

I believe it is my job as the barn owner to educate and reassure all at the same time and I need to earn the trust from all my boarders. Sometimes the trust comes fast and once in a while it takes a long time.

There are always going to be different opinions about mixed herds and I really believe there is so much more to the equation. You have to do what is best for your horse farm but if you are going to mix your herds with your client's horses then I encourage you to really watch them and their personalities for any changes that might lead to problems.

Remember, it is one thing if your own horse gets hurt but if your boarder's horse gets hurt in a situation that could have been avoided, you will be the one picking up the pieces and you might lose a boarder and that is bad for your business.

If you are going to board horses, I strongly encourage you to make sure you have plenty of paddocks which will allow you flexibility. Horses have very individual personalities and having the flexibility to change a horse now and then when a problem arises will make your job so much easier.

Mixed herds can work with careful planning

Whether you decide to have mixed herds at your barn or not is completely your decision and I believe with careful planning and a watchful eye on the horses in your care, mixed herds can work out fine in some situations. Not everyone will agree with mixed herds and you need to be okay with that if you are going to combine your horses.

At the end of the day you need to do what is best for your barn and as long as you can stand behind your decision but be willing to make changes if need be, then this part of barn management will become easier the longer you do it.

It is great to be able to decide how you want your horse business to operate but having a plan "B" in place for those unexpected circumstances is vital for a healthy boarding operation. If you are going to work with horses then you will have the unexpected more often than you ever dreamed. It is a big part of the job especially when it comes to horses. Take the time to learn from those unexpected circumstances and each time will become easier to handle.

Chapter 44

No Two Horses Are the Same

I believe one of the worst things a barn owner can do for their business is to treat every horse exactly the same. I grew up boarding horses and I have been on the down side of a boarding barn that treats all horses the same with no regard to age, breed and size.

I remember a young horse my parents bought me when I was fifteen years old. She was an Appendix Quarter Horse. She was part Thoroughbred and part Quarter Horse and when I took ownership of her she was only fifteen months old. Even at her young age you could tell she was going to be very tall.

I was very young and didn't know anything about nutrition and I must admit I really didn't care. After all how many young kids want to learn about nutrition and how much a horse needs to eat to keep weight on? We boarded her at a stable not to far my home and everything was great.

I was impatiently waiting for the time when I could start riding her and the months went by slow. After about six or seven months I had someone come to me and tell me that my horse was losing too much weight and I needed to talk with the barn owners and ask them to increase the hay. It was the first time that my eyes were open to how thin she was. I couldn't see it before and neither could my parents.

I went to the barn owner that day and told him that I was concerned with the weight loss of my horse and I asked him to increase the hay. He told me that they only feed two flakes of hay twice a day no matter the age, breed or size of the horse. That is what they offered at their stable. Shortly after that I moved her to a new place that included as much hay as she needed to get her weight back up and she started to look much better.

I think about that mare even now

Once you go through something like that you never forget and I still remember that experience like it was yesterday. I think about that mare many times while I am feeding the young horses at my barn and now I make sure I treat each horse on an individual basis and feed them according to their needs.

One misconception or fear that I believe many barn owners have is that if you have huge Draft Horses or Warmbloods at your barn you are going to lose money because they eat so much. There are barn owners that charge more for board due to the extra cost of the hay. I have had many Drafts and Warmbloods at my barn and I have never needed to charge more for hay.

You need to remember that you are going to have small horses and large horses and it will all even out if you let it. The same would be true for ponies that are boarded at your barn. I don't charge less for ponies that are stabled at my barn and they eat a lot less than a horse.

Don't make it complicated

If you start charging according to how much hay a horses is eating, then you will also need to charge accordingly for young horses that are growing and old horses that don't eat as much hay. I talked to one barn owner that charges less for young horses because she says they eat less. I really don't agree with this way of doing things and where do you draw the line? What about the elderly horse that only eats a small amount of hay because he has lost many of his teeth? It can become very complicated and it puts a ton more work on you when it comes to taking care of the paperwork for the board fees. Keep it simple and it will all work out.

Horses and weather

I hear many stories of how barn owners will treat all the horses in their care the same no matter what the weather or temperatures are. The hardy horses do great but it can wear down a horse that is older or thin skinned and doesn't grow a heavy coat. It can even be hard on a horse that is mentally fragile.

Some people have the belief that if you throw them out in any kind of weather or herd situation they will adjust and it will toughen them up. I have seen this go both ways. Sometimes a horse does figure it out and will adjust to the elements and herd setting and once in a while it can make them much more stressed.

This is where a strong and knowledgeable barn owner will keep a watchful eye on the fragile horse and make decisions and changes according to how the horse is doing. Sometimes all it takes is putting a blanket on during the cold months and sometimes it means changing herds to find a better suited herd. I truly believe that if you treat each horse individually and help them along once in a while, they will flourish once they figure out they are safe and they can keep themselves warm and dry.

I hear similar stories often about horses that are struggling at the current barn they are living at when potential new clients come to our place for a tour. It is very frustrating for the boarder when they feel they have no options. I remember those days so clearly and those same feelings come back to me when a person shares some of the issues they are having where they board.

Make a difference

If you want to set your barn apart and make a difference in the life of the horses in your care, then do not treat them all the same. They are not the same at all and you cannot care for a Miniature Horse the same way you would a Draft Horse. It doesn't work. Can it be more work at times? Of course it can and it probably will. Is it worth it once you find a good fit? You bet!

Don't follow what other barns are doing. Set your standards higher for the horses at your farm and watch your business grow and people will notice and talk. You will earn the reputation of having great care and happy horses. Don't forget why you got into this business to begin with. Because you love horses and you want the best for them.

Chapter 45

What Kind Of Clients and Horses Are You Trying To Attract?

If you are just in the beginning stages of building your barn or are already running a farm, one of the most important elements of a successful horse business is knowing what type of clients you want at your barn and what kind of clients and horses would be a good fit for your facility. What you want and what would be a good fit might be on the opposite ends of the spectrum at times.

You might not think these things are important but they truly are especially if you are operating a boarding barn. Our barn is a multi-discipline barn and it is a great place for most disciplines but the footing in our indoor arena is not the best footing for running speed or doing intensive training with reining horses.

I am very upfront with people when they come to see our barn and they want to do speed events or reining. Our outdoor arenas are great for speed and reining but the problem is that we have a very long winter and the outdoor arenas cannot be used when there is a foot of snow on the ground.

If you want to attract trail riders or people that show horses that is great but be prepared because each will need special amenities that you may or may not have. If you want to attract people that jump and turn your barn into primarily a hunter/jumper barn then you will want to spend some extra money on jumps for your indoor and outdoor arena.

If you don't have any idea of what kind of clients you want to attract then I encourage you to take some time and really think about what each discipline needs for amenities and you can offer those amenities as part of your facility. If you have the amenities for a certain riding discipline then there is a good chance you will bring in those types of riders.

Build it and they will come

If you are starting out as a brand new business and money is an issue, try to find out what you can delay buying and take the extra money and purchase some of the things that a riding discipline might need. If you buy used that will work just as good and you will save a lot of money. If you do this at the beginning soon the word will spread and you will start to attract the clients that you want for a certain riding discipline. Remember-build it and they will come!

When we opened, we didn't care what kind of clients or horses came to our barn. We were just happy to fill the stalls! After a few years in business our barn has changed as far as riding disciplines. Early on some of the primary disciplines at our barn were dressage and saddle seat and now we have more huntseat and jumping. We do have many trail and western riders and that has always been popular with so many people. I enjoy watching all the different riding disciplines and it makes for a great learning environment for everyone.

Attracting nice and responsible clients?

When barn owners think about attracting clients to their barn, they always think about the riding disciplines that would be a good fit for their barn. Equally important is attracting responsible clients that pay their board bills and are honest and considerate. This is something most barn owners don't think about when it comes to their business.

As business owners we put such huge pressure on ourselves to keep our stalls filled and many times we will overlook bad behavior from a client just because we need the money. It is a terrible place to be in as a barn owner yet many of us have been there at one time or another.

One of the things many new boarders tell me when they first come to our barn is that they can't believe there is no drama. They are usually surprised at how nice everyone is and how helpful they are. The atmosphere is positive and people are very willing to help each other. We very rarely have someone that is late with their board payment. We have only had two times when someone skipped out without paying their board and both those times were in the first two years of our business.

No more bad stuff allowed

In our early years we had the whole mix of bad stuff happening at our barn. We had drama, people that were not nice at all and boarders that were constantly late on their board payment. As I started to learn how to run a barn and what I wanted in a positive atmosphere with clients, I started to change the atmosphere of the barn by not allowing this negative stuff to go on any more.

I decided it was not going to be tolerated at all in our barn. As I changed as a barn owner and put a stop to all the negative things that were going on, many of the people who live for drama and were the cause of so many negative actions left and moved their horses. This changed our barn in ways that I couldn't imagine at the time.

That is when we started attracting nice people that wanted a barn that was drama free. Our reputation started to grow in a positive "No drama" type of way and wonderful new boarders came to our barn that made our barn a much better place.

No more late board payments

If you want clients that pay their board bill on time, then it is up to you as the barn owner to set the rules about the board payment and then enforce them if a client is constantly late with board. It is never fun to talk with a person about the board and why it is late but as a barn owner you need to do this for your business and your sanity. It does no good to sit up in your house and get upset because you haven't been paid for the board and it is late.

If you want clients that pay their board bill on time, then it is up to you as the barn owner to set the rules about the board payment and then enforce them if a client is constantly late with the board.

You need to be very professional and very direct and once you do this a few times, you won't have a problem in most cases. The last thing your boarders want is a discussion from you about the board. If they know you will address it every month if it is late, they will start paying on time to avoid the conversation all together. Remember the old saying, *the squeaky wheel get the grease.* It is so true!

Once in a while you are going to get a client that loses a job or something bad has happened in their life and you will need to decide how you want to handle it if they are late with the board or worse can't pay it for several weeks. For the most part if you are attracting people that care about paying on time and treating others with respect, then when something bad happens (like a layoff or death in the family) you are able to handle it much better because you know the person is normally a very responsible client. They are just are in a tough spot for a short period of time and they will pay their board as soon as they can.

Set your standards high

There is a huge difference between someone that is a great client and is going through a tough time for the moment and someone who is a dead beat! Once you start earning a reputation for high standards and honest people at your barn, you will not have to worry about the dead beat that wants to keep his horse at your barn for free. They usually don't come because they know they are going to be figured out very fast and it will not be tolerated. They soon will find another barn to leach off of.

Attracting clients to your barn is easy once you know exactly what kind of barn you want on the inside and the outside. Set the standards high for what you want and it will happen.

Chapter 46

You're Clientele Will Change as Your Business Grows. Are You Ready?

Many people that get into horse boarding as a business start off just like we did. They have a farm and own a couple of horses and before you know it they are boarding one or two of their friend's horses. Things seem pretty easy at this stage and then you start to dream about staying at home and boarding horses for a living. The next week you find yourself at the bank applying for a business loan and the rest is history. It happens a lot and the whole idea of having your own business seems like a dream come true. As you go from a couple of horses in your backyard to running a professional boarding facility, there is going to be a huge change in your clientele.

Many people that casually board horses at their home usually have boarders that like to go on trail rides and ride other disciplines on a more casual basis. Some may show and ride year round but people that are very serious about showing and competing usually will find a barn that has a trainer or two and a place that has all the amenities so they can compete at a higher level year round. Most private homes (except for a few) don't offer many of those extra amenities and most do not have trainers on site. We were no different before we built or barn and started our business.

Are you ready? I wasn't at all

We boarded a couple of horses that belonged to our friends and life was easy and good. After we built our twenty-five thousand square foot barn and indoor arena, our life changed and so did our clientele. My first call for boarding was from a big name trainer in the area that wanted to reserve seventeen stalls! I was in shock at the time. All of a sudden I had many trainers and people calling and even though I had people call me that liked to trail ride, I now was talking with many people that competed on the show circuit at a very competitive level. I was entering into a new world of people and clientele.

My clientele was changing very fast and with those changes, the demands of some of those people were intense. They had some strong personalities that I had to learn how to handle as the barn owner and manager. Over the years and through trial and error I have learned to handle any kind of client that comes to my barn. Whether he is a big name trainer or a person that loves to trail ride, I treat them all the same and I don't have the anxiety or issues I used to have. It is definitely something that takes time getting used to and everyone goes through it when they start out in the horse industry.

Remember, you are not alone and many people go through this change of clientele and the anxiety that can come with it. Take it one day at a time and it will get easier as your confidence grows.

Your board rate will attract certain people

One thing many people don't think about is the importance of your board rate and how it will attract certain people to your barn. The truth is if you only charge one hundred dollars for board then most people that have owned a horse for a while will assume that you probably don't have much for extra amenities and a hundred dollars only provides a place to keep a horse with food, shelter and not much more. People that own horses know how expensive they are and a hundred dollars will not get you much for extras at any barn.

If you have a farm and just want a couple of horses to board and nothing more than that rate will probably work. You won't make much money but you will have some help if you want to go away for the weekend and make some new friends. That is exactly how we started.

Getting serious about making a profit

When you get serious and really want to make a profitable business of boarding horses, then as you build and add amenities it is only natural that your board rate is going to increase. Your clientele will change because not everyone can afford a higher end facility so you will be mostly boarding horses that belong to people that make a good income. Some of them will become your friends but for many of them it will be purely a business arrangement and you need to understand this and respect it. It is all part of running a business.

The transition can be hard at first and I must admit that I had a difficult time our first year. I have talked with a couple of barn owners in the past year that have struggled with the changes of clientele at their barn because the people that came were only there to ride and not socialize.

It is so important to understand that not all your clients are going to be your close friends. Many of them will board at your barn because you offer the amenities they need to compete or show at a serious level and that is great. You should embrace it and be happy they are at your barn. Accept them and the situation and realize that they are probably very nice people and if you give it time they will be some of the best boarders you will ever have.

Remember that these people come to your barn because you run a professional facility. They don't want to go to a hobby farm and you are no longer running a hobby farm. Once you embrace this transition and take ownership as a professional your job as a barn owner or manager will become so much easier.

The upper-end barn and your responsibility

I am going to be totally honest and tell you that if you want an upper-end barn where the board is more expensive then you need to be willing to keep up your end of the deal even on days that you don't feel like it. It doesn't mean just cleaning stalls and feeding hay. It also means keeping the arenas groomed and watered if need be. It means that you are going to offer some extra amenities that are kept in good condition and are safe to use. People that are willing to pay more for board are expecting a well-run facility with extras that less expensive places don't offer.

If you advertise that you clean the water buckets then do it and no matter what you charge, keep the water tanks and buckets filled! They should not have to come out to the barn and see green moss growing in their water bucket or find their horse's water bucket empty. It means that extra care is put into the details of your barn program and that also includes taking a good look at each horse on a daily basis. Communicating and letting the customers know what is going on so they don't have to guess is all part of a well-run boarding facility. These are things that should be done at any size barn or facility and it should have nothing to do with the price of the board.

The expectations are higher

It is true that the expectations of an upper-end barn are going to be higher and that is expected. It is no different than you buying a very expensive car and expecting it to have more features. You are not going to spend fifty thousand on an automobile and it doesn't come with air-conditioning or a CD player. It's just not going to happen.

The most important thing to remember is that your clients work hard for their money and they deserve to get what they are paying for. If you are going to run a barn then be honored that they have chosen your barn to bring their horse to.

You have the wonderful opportunity to meet many different types of people from all walks of life at your barn. I encourage you to embrace each one of them and their horses. I have met and made friends with people that I would have probably never met otherwise and it has been the greatest experience. Don't miss out on the wonderful opportunity of making new friends that is right in front of you.

Chapter 47

What Is So Important About a Clean Barn Anyway?

We are slobs! Well as least many of us are at times and I am no exception. Keeping things clean is a lot of work and keeping a barn clean with many horses and people using it all day long is never ending.

I am very blessed to have a husband that is very meticulous about keeping everything clean and in its place and that has transferred to our barn. If you were to ask any boarder past or present that has been at our barn, I know without a doubt that they would tell you our barn is always extremely clean. I'm not bragging at all but I want to share why I feel it is important to have a clean barn and how it will make your business better and stand out among other barns.

The dirty barn

We all have been to dirty barns. I have boarded at barns that were not kept up and I have walked through some barns that were so filthy that I wondered how you could find anything. The feeling you get when you are in a barn that is not clean is usually not good. Many people board at barns that are dirty and a real mess because they have the belief that horses are animals and it doesn't really matter to them.

Well to some degree the horse doesn't care if stuff is lying around all over the place but I have a different outlook on why a clean barn is better for all including the horses.

Mud vs. filthy

As you know horses love to roll in the mud and get dirty and they could care less if they have not been brushed in a few days. There is a big difference between a horse rolling in the mud and getting a little dirty and walking into a barn that is filthy and stinks and the urine burns your eyes.

There is also something to be said about a barn that has junk lying around everywhere. It's a safety hazard for you but also more importantly it's a safety hazard for all the horses in your care. If you are running a barn and you have stuff lying around everywhere, there is a very good chance a horse will get into it and get hurt at one time or another. Why even take the chance when you don't have to.

I am going to be very honest and tell you right now that if a client's horse gets hurt because of all the junk that is lying around at your barn, that client is going to be upset with you and the fall-out could be even worse. They might want you to pay for the injury and there is a good chance you will lose a boarder. It is not good for your business and not good at all for your reputation.

Keep it clean

If you are going to run a barn and you want to attract a certain clientele then keep your barn clean. People will notice and it will increase the value of your facility without any extra cost to you but some labor. If you expect people to pay a monthly board bill then give them a clean barn with everything in its place because they deserve that.

If you expect people to pay a monthly board bill then give them a clean barn with everything in its place because they deserve that.

Make it a habit

The funny thing is once you start making it a habit to keep your barn clean, your boarders will appreciate it and many of them will help keep it clean. We have wonderful boarders that go above and beyond the call of duty to help keep our barn and lounge extra clean. Your clients will get to the point where they won't accept anything less. They will start taking the time to make sure everything is in its place and together your barn will stay clean all the time.

A clean barn is great for business and it is healthier for the horses. In a world where many people don't take pride in their jobs or barns anymore, set your place apart by just keeping it clean and everything in its place. It will make a huge difference in your business and remember a clean barn tells people that you care. That speaks volumes alone about you and your horse business.

Chapter 48

Boundaries

I cannot express enough how important boundaries are between you and your clients. This was something I needed to learn when we first opened up our barn and I had some hard lessons trying to figure out where the boundaries were between me and my boarders.

Once you become a business owner your role is going to change and most people are not fully ready for the change when it happens. Becoming a business owner is something that not everyone is cut out for. It means you become the boss and no one can prepare you for that position until you are in it and living it daily at your job.

Finding the boundaries between my clients and me took many years to figure out. I didn't have anyone to mentor me through the process and so I had to learn the hard way as many situations came up. Many of the mistakes I made were because I tried too hard to be close friends with everyone and I wanted to know everything about them. I had not learned at the time that this was business and my boarders just wanted to come out and ride. Not all of them wanted to have a close friendship with the barn owner.

Sharing too much

Another big mistake I make many times in our early years was that I shared too much about the business and problems with the barn to many boarders. I am going to tell you right now that is a huge mistake!

The first thing you need to remember above all else is that you are running a business and there are many things that go on that should never be discussed with your clients. Not only is it unprofessional but it puts them in an uncomfortable position especially if you are complaining about another client or you are talking about your money issues.

Your clients pay a lot of money to have a horse and to keep it at your barn. If you start spilling your guts to them about your financial stress they are going to start to worry about the future of your barn and their horse. Their number one concern is their horse and if they hear you are having financial problems, they will start to wonder if you are going to have enough money to buy hay, bedding or pay the bills.

You may be thinking this doesn't happen but let me tell you it does and it happens all the time. There are boarding barns all over that go bankrupt and the boarders are stuck trying to find hay for their horse and a new place to board and that is without a moment's notice.

I would strongly encourage you to find someone that is not directly involved with horses in your immediate area and who you trust, and talk with them about the problems you are facing. It truly needs to be someone that is not involved with your barn so they can give you an honest view of what they see and then you can make clear decisions.

Boundaries are for everyone including barn owners!

One of the mistakes I made the first couple of years running our barn was trying to become friends with everyone. I like people and I wanted them to like me and I wanted to know all about them personally. I didn't have proper boundaries set and I am sure I made a few people uncomfortable.

I can remember one specific time when we had a very nice woman that boarded at our barn and she was extremely quiet. She was a great boarder and came out to ride a lot but what I didn't realize was that she came out to the barn for quiet time. She didn't want to talk with others at all and she just wanted to enjoy her horse. She had a very stressful job around people all day long so when she came to the barn in the evening the last thing she wanted to do was talk to people.

I was so stupid at the time and I let it bother me because she didn't want to socialize with anyone. I didn't get it until one day she talked with me and told me about her job and all the stress and then she started to tell me about the stress she was having in her personal life. I finally got it! The barn was her place to unwind and find peace and I was not making it peaceful for her at all because I was always trying to include her in everything.

I understand now

After that talk I finally learned that not everyone wants to ride with others and not everyone wants to go out for dinner after a ride and that is okay. I had to remember that even though I am here on the farm every day, most people go to a job and work all day and then come to the barn. Some of your clients are not going to be social people that want to be involved with all the activities of your barn. That is okay and you need to remember this otherwise you might lose a wonderful boarder because you made them feel uncomfortable at the time.

This woman that I was talking about earlier was one of the best boarders we have ever had and I was very sad the day she moved her horse to a smaller and less busy barn, but I was truly happy for her. She found a barn that was a better fit and now as I have become a little older and a little smarter I completely understand.

As you start to run your business you will learn to read people and you need to be very aware that each person is different. You will have some clients that love to socialize and talk for hours and you will have some that come ride their horse and leave without talking with anyone. It takes all types to make a great barn. It is important to be accepting of all your clients and be respectful of their space and time when they come to see their horse.

The boarder that doesn't respect boundaries

You are also going to have the other extreme when you have a business. It is the boarder that doesn't know their boundaries when it comes to your personal life and your family. I have had a couple of boarders over the years that really didn't have an understanding or respect for boundaries.

Having a working farm with horses and people at your place can be hard once in a while and most of your clients will understand this but there are going to be a few that don't. We have had a couple of boarders over the years that have walked right into our home without knocking. I have had clients ride their horse right up to our living room window while we were eating dinner and stare into the window. I have had clients call me as late as eleven o'clock at night and knock on our door as early as eight in the morning on a Sunday. Now I completely understand if it is an emergency but in each of these cases it was not at all.

You will have to find what you feel comfortable with and set your boundaries from there. It is perfectly fine to address a situation if you feel a client is over stepping their boundaries. I believe that if you talk with the person in a respectful way and be honest, they will understand and in most cases it won't happen again.

You might need to be direct

If you find yourself in a position where a client keeps crossing the line of what is acceptable at your barn, you will need to be very direct and it might mean saying, "Please do not come into my home without knocking first. This is our home and we want to keep it separate from the business." Some people just need to have it explained as direct as possible. I have never had a person leave our barn because I was too direct with them about boundaries. Usually I will address the situation and the issue is resolved.

Over the years people have lost their sense of what boundaries are in this world. You can go on Facebook and people will say anything about anyone with no regards to how it can affect the person they are talking about. When it comes to your barn you will need to be the one that sets the boundaries and even though it might be uncomfortable at first, you will get used to your role and I can promise you that later on you will be thankful you did.

Boundaries are essential for keeping a business healthy and strong and if you are not sure where to start then I you encourage you to talk with someone that has run a successful horse business and can give you some sound honest advice. They will help you through those learning situations that we all go through.

Boundaries are essential for keeping a business healthy and strong.

Chapter 49

Extra Charges for Services Done

If you are not sure what to charge or when to charge for services done, then you are not alone. Many barn owners I talk with have the same questions and deciding what you want to charge your clients can become confusing if you don't have a clear definition of what your "extra services" are.

A great starting place to find out what kind of services you want to charge for is by talking with other barn owners and see what extra services they offer at their barn. It doesn't mean you need to do exactly what they are doing but it does give you a foundation to start with.

The most important questions you should ask is why they offer the services they do and what their fee is for each service. Every barn is going to be a little different on what they offer for services and the size of your barn and number of horses will play a huge part on the services offered at your barn.

Everything is easier with only two or three

If you only have three boarders then putting on blankets and taking them off will not be a big deal at all and you probably will have no problem changing blankets for free. If you have a lot of horses at your barn then it will be a full time job in itself (I am exaggerating a little). Blanketing can take up much of your time and you will get tired very quickly of doing it for free.

The same will go for many other services you offer at your farm. Two or three horses is never a big deal but once you start doing extra services for ten horses or more, you will quickly see how much time it takes and that is time taken away from other things that need to get done. If you are running an equine business you will soon realize that time is money and they are connected on many levels.

What services do you want to offer?

The first thing you need to decide is what services are going to be included in your regular board rate and what will the fee be for extra services. If you talk a few barn owners they will all give you a different spin on how they do it. I think it is very smart to talk to as many barn owners as possible and then that will give you a good feel for what is being done in your area and it will give you many ideas on where to start at your barn.

There are barns that include services like blankets and medications as part of the board but you need to understand that their board is probably higher than other barns. If a barn owner is a smart business person, he is not going to give away his services and time for free. He will include blanketing as part of his regular board fee but his rate will be higher to compensate him for his time. The reality is time is money and if you spend an extra hour each day putting on and taking off blankets, that is seven hours a week that you could have been doing something else. It adds up very quickly.

If a barn owner is a smart business person, he is not going to give away his services and time for free.

At our barn we have our regular board rate and then add extra fees for special services provided. It gives my boarders options on how much they want to spend. In most cases at our barn, our boarders will find a friend to do blanket duty with them and they exchange services between each other. It saves them money each month and it works out for everyone involved.

I also have a few boarders that would rather pay me to put on and take off blankets and I charge them accordingly and they are happy to have the service. Giving your boarders a few options is great for your business and your clients.

Your extra services will change

The one thing for sure, no matter where you start in this area of offering services at your barn, you will most likely modify it and make changes as time goes along. I used to charge a lot more for many extra services (like fly masks) because I envisioned having to put on forty fly masks each day and take all of them off every evening. I really thought at the time it was going to be very time consuming. After I had been running our barn for a few years, I realized that putting on a few fly masks was not a big deal at all and I stopped charging a fee for the service.

Sometimes all it takes is time and experience to see what is going to be easy and what is going to be more work than what you expected. Be open to change because it will happen.

Over the years I have had many barn owners ask me what our extra services sheet looks like so I thought I would include it in this book. Remember, my examples are not the only way to offer services but this is how I have done it for years and it has worked out well.

Extra Services offered

1. Private turnout-$10.00 per week

If you have a boarding barn then you are going to need some kind of private turnout. As long as you have horses on your property, you will have a horse now and then that is lame and needs a quiet area to mend or someone that wants private turnout for their show horse. There are many reasons why someone will want private turnout and if you want to make your job easier then take the time to create a few spots for private turnout. Private turnout does create extra work for the barn owner and it should come with a fee. At most barns it is not part of the normal amenities offered with the regular board fee.

2. Stall fans-$10.00 per month. Fan must be approved before it is hung up.

I want to start off by saying that we don't charge for stall fans anymore but we did for many years. During the first few years of our business, I wasn't really sure how expensive it was going to be to have twenty-seven fans going and I was worried our electric bill was going to go through the roof.

After a few years I had a good idea of the cost and I decided that we could offer this service for free. It was a great perk for our boarders and I think they appreciated it. The electric fees might be different in your area so you will want to have a good idea of how much it will cost to run fans before you offer it for free. Our boarders were always very happy to pay the ten dollars a month and they were just happy that we allowed fans to begin with since many barns don't have the electric capabilities.

3. Boots (on/off)-$15.00 per month

I have only had two times in the last ten years where I needed to put boots on every morning before I put a horse outside. I have never charged because it turned out not to be a big deal at all. I have always kept this in my service sheet so that I am covered if a situation comes up where I need to put on boots for many horses on a daily basis. Putting the boots on is easy part. It is taking them off when they are covered in mud that is a real pain. It is just something to think about.

4. Blanketing (on/off)-$1.00 per day

Blanketing is something that can be easy or it can be complicated. It really depends on the owner and what type of blankets they own. I do blanketing for a couple of horses in our barn and I have guidelines for all the owners that use blankets. They must be in good condition with all the straps and clips working. They also must use a blanket that fits correctly. It is not fun to put a blanket on a horse that is too small and too tight.

I do not charge a lot for blanketing but I do charge what I feel it is worth for me to do this service. I know plenty of barns that charge more for this service and you will need to do what works best for you when it comes to blanketing.

5. Fly Mask (on/off)-fifty cents per day

We don't charge for putting on fly masks any more. We used to when we first opened because I was worried that I was going to have to put on forty fly masks everyday which would have been a lot of extra work. It turns out that very few people use fly masks and I dropped the fee years ago. It really takes no time to put one on but when we first opened I was overwhelmed and any extra job seemed like a big deal at the time.

I do let my boarders know if their fly mask is full of mud because I will not wash it out and I will not put it back on the horse if they can't see out of it properly. If you decide you want to provide the service of washing out the fly mask you might want to adjust your rates accordingly.

6. Holding Fee (Vet/Farrier)-$10.00 per time

I have known barns to charge more for this service and I do believe it depends on the area you live in. Some barns also charge in thirty minute increments. This rate is easy to adjust and you might need to adjust it as time goes on.

7. Giving Wormer-$10.00 per time

I give our boarders a choice on our deworming program but it must follow what the veterinarians are recommending as a guideline. I have had boarders that do not feel comfortable worming their horse so they will pay me to administer it. I charge enough to cover the cost of the wormer and my time. It works out great for the clients that want that option and you will probably have few people that will want you to give it.

Extra Charges for Rehabilitation/Lay-up Fees (Veterinarian Prescribed)

1. Simple Medicating-Any medication given at times other than scheduled feedings-$2.00 per time.

2. Walking Fee-$10.00/per walk (10-15 minutes)

3. Hosing Fee-$10.00/per session (10-15 minutes)

4. Bandaging Fee-$2.00 per leg

5. Misc. Fees-To be determined depending on the service

6. Material, Supplies, Medication Fee-To be determined

Please remember that these are just some examples of what we charge extra fees for. You have the ability to decide what you want to charge for and how much for the service. There are going to be services that you feel need to charge more for and others that you want to offer for next to nothing or free.

You are also going come across requests for services that you may have never thought of before. You will need to think about a rate if you are going to provide the service and after you provide that service you might modify the fee for the future. It could be something like washing horses and clipping services.

One more important thought-As a barn owner or manager you might find yourself having a hard time charging your clients fees for services provided. It happens to almost all new horse professionals and it happened to me. The truth is that if you don't charge for some of these services like blanketing then you will find yourself doing more and more of it. There is a good chance you will burn yourself out and you will regret your decision to not charge a fee.

I don't want to do this service!

There are going to be services that you don't want to do and no amount of money is worth it. If you come across a service that is requested and you don't want to provide it then you need to be very honest with your client right from the start. Some services are not worth the money when it takes up too much of your time.

You need to remember that your day is already extremely long and it will get even longer if you can't say no. Even if you say yes and you are making extra money, you might find yourself becoming irritated every day when you have to provide the service. Sometimes it is far better to say no in the beginning and be done with it.

My services have changed over the years and I now give more services for free than we did in the beginning. Some services I will always charge for but many of them were not as time consuming as I imagined. You will go through this also and you can adjust your services according to what works for you and your schedule.

Chapter 50

The Difference Between the Barn Owner and Barn Manager

When we first opened our boarding barn I really didn't have a clear idea of what my title or role was in our new business. I was doing it all and I didn't give it any more thought in those early years of running our business. A few years ago I started to really think about the role a barn owner has and the role of a barn manager.

There are many people that own a barn and they are also the barn manager. Then there are barn owners that hire a full time barn manager to run the barn and keep everything going.

I really think it is important to define each role and their importance to each other because a barn will start to have problems due to a conflict between the barn owner and barn manager. Many times the barn owner doesn't like some of the decisions the barn manager is making or the barn manager doesn't like some of the decisions that the barn owner will make for the business. It goes both ways and it can get messy.

I have talked with a few barn owners that are stressed because they don't know how to put boundaries on what their barn manager is allowed to do. They don't have a clear vision of what they want for their barn so the result is that the barn manager has no direction and no boundaries. It is simply a problem of vision and communication.

It can be equally as frustrating for the barn managers because they are trying to do the best job they can with what they have to work with. If they are working for a barn owner that doesn't want to make much needed changes then the barn manager will become frustrated and eventually burn out. Both roles are so very important and both need to have the same vision or the barn won't run as well as it should.

The barn owner

The barn owner is the person that pays the bills and many times will have a huge business mortgage. That alone puts them in a class by themselves. The barn owner carries the weight of everything that happens on the farm. They know that if things are not running as they should, they will lose clients and the end result is always loss of income.

If the money is not coming in then it becomes much harder to pay everything that needs to be paid and that includes the barn manager. There is a ton of pressure that comes with being the barn owner and until you are in those shoes you will never fully understand that feeling.

Many barn owners will manage their own barn but there are many that are in a financial position where they can hire a full-time barn manager. If the barn owner has another job that brings in income, he might hire a barn manager to keep things running while he is away at work. Each barn owner will have different goals and desires for his barn. Whether it is a boarding facility, breeding barn, racing barn or any other horse stable, the bottom line is the barn owner does not want to lose money on his investment.

The bottom line is the financials

The barn owner will always look at everything that involves his barn as an investment because he is the one paying all the bills and his farm is an investment that he does not want to lose. It might sound cold to many people but the reality is the barn owner needs to look at his horse facility and how it is run in a financial way and it becomes so much more than just about the horses. It is a business first.

I am a barn owner and I love the horses on our farm but I still look at everything from a business stand point. Every time a horse pulls down the fence or kicks in a corner feeder, someone needs to fix it and with that comes the expense. The barn manager will not feel the frustration with this part of the business because they do not need to worry about the bills. They might empathize and understand if they were at one time a barn owner themselves but they won't feel the pressure or stress.

The reason the direction and goals of a barn owner might be a little different than the barn manager is because they are usually making decisions from a financial point of view. They don't have the luxury to make poor decisions based on a dream they have. They need facts and numbers before they can take a chance and try something new that might cost them a lot of money especially if it doesn't work out.

People think we are rich!

I believe barn owners are very often misjudged. When people drive up to our farm and see our barn, the first thing a few people have said to me is, "Boy, you must be bringing in the money to have a barn like this!" When they say that statement to me it always gets under my skin a little. They don't realize how much our mortgage is or how expensive it is to keep a farm going. I believe people assume David and I are doing quite well but they don't have any idea of the huge expense it takes to run any farm.

Barn owners will always meet people that don't have a clear understanding of what it cost to keep a farm going. As the barn owner it is important for you to make sure to hire a barn manager that has some idea of the expense to run a farm. It might mean sitting down with them and sharing some of the financials so they have a very clear understanding of where you are coming from. If you take the time to share this with your barn manager, it will help your working relationship more than you will ever know.

The barn manager

If you are in a financial position to hire a barn manager then I encourage you to do it, even if it is part-time a couple days a week. Having a barn manager to take some of the load off is invaluable and finding a good barn manager that understands how to communicate with people is a gem for sure.

I believe there are a lot of great and knowledgeable barn managers out there that can be a true asset to a barn but one of the issues that many of them face is that they don't have a clear definition of what their job duties are.

They probably will have the authorization to make decisions about horse nutrition or rehab for an injured horse but if they see an area that needs improving or would work better if done a different way, they usually need to get it approved first by the barn owner. If they work for a barn owner that is never out in the barn or is closed minded it can become very frustrating for the barn manager especially if the barn owner says no to every new idea that is suggested.

The barn manager's role will vary greatly depending on what kind of barn they work at. They really won't know how much authority they will have running the barn until they do it for a while and prove themselves as a knowledgeable equine professional.

I believe the most successful barn managers are the ones that not only are well educated about horses and horse care but they are also equally wise about people and how to take care of the clients at their barn. They are great with communicating and know how to lead and are confident in the decisions they need to make, even when a client will not be happy about it.

Different visions

Over the last couple of years I have talked with a few barn owners that were frustrated because their barn manager didn't have the same vision they did. They liked everything the barn manager was doing for the care of the horses, but it was constantly a tug-o-war between the barn owner and manager on the direction the farm was going. The same complaint has been said from the barn manager's point of view. The biggest problem is communication between the two and understanding the pressure each one feels.

If you are going to run a successful barn as the barn owner or barn manager then the most important thing to work towards is a common goal and vision for the barn.

Each role whether as barn owner or barn manager needs to be defined and as the barn owner, you need to learn to trust and not micro-manage if your barn manager is doing a great job. As the barn manager, you need to make sure you don't overstep your bounds and if you want to make changes, you need to understand that the barn owner will always look at it first from a financial point of view.

Once each person comes to an understanding and respects and trusts the other and what they can do for the horses and clients then your barn and business will only get better from there.

Great with horses, terrible with people!

It is so important to remember that it doesn't matter how good your barn manager is with horses if he is terrible with people. If he is great with organization and has a great work ethic, but he is short-tempered with your clients it will hurt your business. If the reason your boarders are leaving your barn is because of your barn manager then as the barn owner you need to reevaluate your situation.

A great barn manager needs to have a balance. Knowledge of horse care is a must but also equally important is a good work ethic, honesty and great people skills. Once you find a barn manager that has those qualities, don't lose them because they are worth their weight in gold!

When you are both the barn owner and barn manager

I believe this is the area most people fall into and I am one of them. I own our barn and I also run it. Most people that build a barn and start boarding horses also manage it themselves. There are a few barns around my area that have a barn manager but it really depends on so much with money as the main factor.

If you own and manage a barn then you know how hard it can be. You become both the financial wizard trying to pull money out of nowhere to fix everything that needs to be fixed and you are also the person that does all the daily chores and oversees the care of the horses. Add on top of it the relationship with your clients and trying to find balance between your roles as the owner and manager. With both those jobs will come many different hats that you will wear and sometimes you will have them all on at the same time.

Find a support system

If you are in this category where you are running the barn and paying the mortgage then I encourage you to find positive people who you can talk through issues with and who can give you sound advice when things are not going good. The position of both barn owner and manager can definitely have its downside with lonely days when you feel like no one understands how you feel. If you find yourself in conflict then that is when you need to go to someone you trust to help you through it.

Many businesses have management and consultants to help make sure the company is staying healthy and sound. In the horse industry you don't usually hear of this practice in too many barns. In fact you really don't hear about it at all. People that own the farm and manage it really need someone to look at the business from the outside and help them develop a positive game plan to improve the barn and the atmosphere and keep the business healthy and strong.

What people need to realize is that you don't need to be a huge breeding barn or boarding facility to have problems. Small barns with only a few horses and clients will have the same issues but just on a smaller scale. No matter the size of your barn, take the time to talk monthly with someone that has more experience in business and customer relations to help grow your business and make it stand out as a great barn.

Being the barn owner and manager is not an easy job but it can become easier the longer you do it. Just remember that no one can do it all by themselves. It truly does take a team (no matter the size) to make it successful.

Chapter 51

Educating Will Be Part of the Job

When we opened our boarding business I had a lot to learn about business and people. Every day was a new experience and I was learning very quickly that educating your clients was part of the job. I now believe it should be part of the job and it is a very important part.

I had boarded my horses for many years when I was younger and I had very few conversations with the barn owners of each stable. Looking back maybe the barn owner should have stepped in when I was having a difficult time because then I wouldn't have made so many mistakes with my horse. I don't know for sure if that is the correct way to look at it but it has made me think about things very differently when it comes to my clients.

I have experienced both sides of the horse world. The client side and the barn owner side and they both have their own set of issues. When we opened our barn for business we were full in one month and my life became crazy. The one thing that caught me off guard was the amount of questions I would receive about the care and nutrition of the horses.

Brand new horse owners

I somehow just assumed that my boarders would need very little help from me about nutrition and basic care but I was very wrong. In fact I never gave this area any thought. The part I was not thinking about at all was that fact that many of my boarders would be brand new horse owners for the first time in their life.

Now let me say first hand that we have been blessed to have had so many new horse owners make our barn their barn home and it has been an honor to help them along the way and watch them grow as horsemen. I now cherish the times when I can help someone but when we were a new business, I was so shell shocked by the whole business world and learning to run our barn that I felt overwhelmed by all the extra questions I was getting at the time.

I was not prepared to educate

It was not the boarders fault at all that they had a lot of questions. It was my fault completely because I was not fully prepared to run a barn at the time and I didn't have the confidence to be educating others as well. I was so worried that I would direct them in the wrong way or I would say something that would offend them, that it became very stressful for me during the first few years.

Every person that owns a horse is always learning and the learning never stops. I embrace that now and I am constantly learning something new at our barn. As I learn, I try to pass that information along to our boarders and help them.

If you are going to run a barn, the first thing you need to remember is that it is not just about taking care of the horses. It is also about taking care of the people and helping them learn and grow as horse owners. I believe a successful barn manager has the skills to educate without making a client feel stupid or inadequate. It takes time to learn those skills and it might involve making a few mistakes along the way as you learn to educate and communicate with your clients in a positive way.

Your clients might have a trainer that they go to a lot with questions and they might even consult with their veterinarian but I guarantee that a few of them will want to ask your opinion about certain issues. The best thing you can do is take the time and talk with them and help them understand what is going on with their horse. They might have questions about something simple like changing grains and supplements and how to make the transition. It could also be something more serious like a bad behavior that they don't know how to correct and they want to know what you think and get your professional advice.

Take each question as a chance to learn how to lead and the more time you spend helping your clients, the more confident you will become as a barn owner and manager. The two go hand in hand and the results will change you and your barn for the better.

Chapter 52

The Financials

Let's be honest about business. The truth is none of us go into business to go bankrupt. If we are going to go through all the time and pain it takes to start a business then we are going to want to be successful at it and make a profit. I know that most of us get into the horse business because we love horses but there is no way of keeping our passion alive if we are not running a healthy business with sound financials. That means we need to have more money coming in than is going out.

I hear many people say that you can't make living boarding horses but I am going to tell you right now that you can but you need to be very smart about it. You may never get rich working in the horse industry but you will have a rich life if you take the time to do it right. You just need to be smart about your money.

You may never get rich working in the horse industry but you will have a rich life if you take the time to do it right. You just need to be smart about your money.

Myths about business

There are a couple of myths that new business owners get themselves into trouble with and sometimes those early mistakes are what put a barn out of business. I have talked with many people, both business owners and non-business owners that have the same belief. They have this idea that if you own a business you can borrow almost any amount of money for anything that has to do with the business and that is perfectly fine. They also believe that if it's a business expense, you can write it off on your taxes so go ahead and spend, spend spend!

Many business owners (especially new business owners) believe that if you are borrowing to buy something for the farm it will not affect your personal income, home or even your life because it is separate from these things. That is not true at all.

What many people don't grasp is that even though you can write off business purchases on your taxes, you still need to pay the monthly bill. What do you do if the monthly bills become too high and you're not bringing in enough money to cover them? This happens more than you would believe and it does affect your business, family and life in many ways.

Too many new business owners believe that in order to look professional to their clients they need everything to be brand new and that idea comes with a heavy price tag. If a person gets themselves in over their head in debt because they borrowed too much for business purchases, it will put an added stress on the person and the business without them realizing it at the time.

Be conservative

Be cautious and conservative when making purchases. Everything might be great at the moment especially if you have a full barn but when a rainy day or year comes, those large payments are going to be very hard to make. The stress it will cause you will eventually trickle into all the other parts of your business and your client's will notice. Money issues are very hard to hide.

I encourage you to be wise when borrowing for a business and leave yourself a cushion in the event that you go through a tough time financially. Most businesses go through lean periods at one time or another. I have never heard anyone say that they regret growing their business slow and usually those businesses are the ones that flourish and last.

I have never heard anyone say that they regret growing their business slow and usually those businesses are the ones that flourish and last.

Don't make the same mistake so many people do. It is so easy to get caught up in the trap and mindset of, "We own a business" and apply for that new business charge card. It becomes too tempting to spend what you don't have. I was there many years ago and I spent way too much money trying to build more and better and it caught up with me fast.

It will eventually catch up with you especially if the income that you are bringing in doesn't match what needs to go out. Take your time and remember slow and steady always wins the race!

The business plan

The best thing you can do for your business is write up a business plan. It doesn't matter if you are borrowing money or not. It will truly give you the best and honest view of your business and how it affects everything your barn is about.

I never understood the value in a business plan until I had to put one together. It took us nine months to prepare it and after it was done I knew so much more about running our business from a financial point. Our business plan truly showed us what it was really going to take to make our barn a financial success.

Remember, it is not just about borrowing money. Business plans are about the inner workings of your business and it helps give you a clear vision and direction for your operation. There is nothing better to give you a solid understanding of your equine business then a detailed, well thought out business plan.

Building a barn and starting a horse business is no small task. If you decide you want to go that route, I applaud you for your courage and I strongly encourage you to write a business plan. Take the time to do it right and go over every part of your horse business all the way down to the brooms and muck buckets you will need to buy. You will never regret it.

Don't be a slave to the lender

The saying is very true, that if you get yourself into extreme debt over your business, you will soon become a slave to the lender. It will make your life that much harder especially when you have to count every penny and you can't afford to hire help because you don't have the extra money.

David and I have been down that path due to many mistakes on our part and it is a very bad place to be. Don't let yourself be fooled into the belief that you can borrow as much as you want because you have a business. Don't be another statistic like many businesses that go under in the first five years. Choose to do things differently with your business and money and you will beat the odds.

Don't be another statistic like many businesses that go under in the first five years. Choose to do things differently with your business and money and you will beat the odds.

You can be the difference in your business and it starts with you. Start slow and grow with your business and your business will grow with you. It will truly make going to work every day so much better.

Chapter 53

Are You Willing to Ask a Boarder to Leave For the Betterment of Your Barn?

When we opened our boarding facility I had never given any thought to asking a boarder to leave. After all why would I need to ask anyone to leave? This is another area where I give you permission to laugh if you want to. David and I were so naive when it came to running a boarding stable and when we first opened I didn't realize we were going to need to make some very tough choices on how we wanted our barn to be.

The first year our barn was in full operation I really loved the work of taking care of the horses. In fact the morning chores were my best part of the day and the easiest. Feeding the horses and cleaning stalls is a great way to start the day on any farm. Our barn opened for clients at 8am every day of the week so by mid-morning the barn was coming to life with people. During those early years I so eager to please and really would do whatever a boarder asked and under almost any circumstance. It was a terrible way to run a business.

How did it get this bad so fast?

It became very clear to a few people at our barn that I was not in control and they felt they could pretty much do anything they wanted. Before I knew it boarders were bringing in strange horses without my permission and using other horse's stalls without the owner's consent. Tack was being used and never put back and in some cases I found boarders that were using others peoples tack without their permission. Very quickly we were having problems in many different areas of our barn and I had no idea how to handle it as I was also very intimidated by some of the strong personalities. The worst was about to come.

What made the entire situation more difficult were a couple of people telling other clients what they could and could not do and basically trying to run the barn. People were talking about each other and tearing each other down. I had boarders calling me upset with hurt feelings and all the drama that goes with it. How did it get so bad so fast?

I had too many people trying to be the boss and I was not acting like a boss at all. I believe now that it is very true, if you don't lead your barn then someone else will. That was the case for us.

David and I finally sat down and really discussed all the problems occurring in the barn and we needed to decide how we were going to fix it. I had to get out of my comfort zone and be the leader and business owner I needed to be and this was unfamiliar territory for me.

Fear of losing boarders

Another piece of the story was the fact that I was scared to death to lose boarders. We were strapped for money and we really needed the income from every single boarder we had. I was very worried that if we couldn't come to an agreement and I asked them to leave I would not be able to fill the empty stalls. We still had bills to pay and a large business mortgage. The stress was huge.

I know now this crosses almost every barn owners mind and it can be a very real fear but it can also cripple a barn if you allow negative people to ruin the atmosphere of your facility.

The first time

Years later I still think about that first time I needed to ask someone to leave. We lost five horses and boarders over that situation but now I think it was the turning point in making me the business person I needed to be to run a healthy barn. In fact it taught me so much that I can even say I am glad it happened now.

It was one of the hardest things I have had to do at our barn but without being forced to take care of the problems in our barn, I would not have grown as a business owner. Sometimes we all need a little push.

We did fill all five stalls pretty quickly and the barn atmosphere changed almost immediately for the better. Wonderful new boarders came to our farm and everything improved daily.

Take a chance and lead

Are you willing to ask a boarder to leave for the betterment of your barn? I sure hope so. The best thing for your barn and business is to earn a good reputation for the care of the horses and also how it is managed. Part of that reputation will be about the atmosphere at your barn. If you are a positive leader and create a "no drama" barn with a positive atmosphere, the word will spread and that is a fantastic reputation to have.

If you lead with positive and fair leadership your clients will respect you and want to stay. You will be surprised at how the word spreads and before you know it you will have a waiting list and much less turnover. It can be done. All you need to do is take a chance and be the leader you know you are inside.

Chapter 54

Habits of Highly Successful Horse Professionals

Do I have your attention? I sure hope so. Over the last few years I have had the pleasure of talking with many people about their boarding operations and I embrace how each one of them are run a little differently.

I have met people that are running successful boarding facilities and then I have met and talked with many people that are struggling. I must admit that I have talked with more people that are struggling than with people that are content and secure with how their barn runs. It can be a tough business to work in but not usually because of the horses. They are almost always the easiest part of the business.

The other part of the equation is that being a successful barn has very little to do with making lots of money. Let's face it, you will not become rich boarding horses and you will probably make less money than you envisioned. What defines a successful horse business to me is not the income that is being brought in each month. Sure we need to pay our bills and make sure we have money in our savings account for unexpected expenses (which will happen) but to me success is much deeper.

I will be the first to say that I believe our barn is successful but it took a few years to get to that point. David and I still owe a huge business mortgage and if you were to look at our lifestyle you would probably wonder how we keep our twenty year old vehicles running day in and day out. Yet I feel blessed that our business is a success and on solid footing.

I believe now that successful horse professionals have many of the same habits that keep their clients coming back. Whether you are a horse trainer, breeder or own a boarding facility, there are core beliefs and work ethics that keep these people at the top of their profession.

I have listed several habits that I believe will change how you run your horse business and it will set your place apart. Remember, learning to be a business owner in a tough industry takes time and it is a journey. We all take two steps forward and one step back at times and as you change from the inside out you will start to see a change in your horse business also.

1. You can't fix a problem until you truly understand the source of the problem.

I have talked with many people over the years that will call me with a problem they are having at their farm. Sometimes when you are the one having the problem it is very hard to see where the problem is stemming from. I admire people that are willing to ask for help and have someone else look at their business from the outside and with fresh eyes. It takes guts to ask for help at times and admit you might not know how to fix the issues at your barn.

I encourage anyone that is having problems to find a person who can look at your business and give you honest feedback. That is the first step to fixing those very challenging issues most barns deal with at one time or another.

2. If you don't lead your barn with confidence then somebody else will.

Running your own business is extremely hard work but it can be even harder if you are not the one in control. As the business owner you need to lead your clients with honesty and integrity. They might not like all your business decisions regarding your barn but if they respect you and believe that you only want the best for them and their horse, it will really change your barn atmosphere.

3. If you are going to do the job then do it well. Don't cut corners!

I believe every person that sets out to start their own business has the best intentions. They are excited and the energy they have is endless. After a while they start to realize the work load is heavy than they thought it would be and they look for ways to cut corners to make the job easier. That is fine if you are looking for ways to be efficient without compromising the care of the horses.

I always tell people if you are going to clean the water buckets then do it well. If you are going to feed hay then feed good quality hay. If you are going to inspect each horse as you walk them in or out of the barn then do it thoroughly. Whatever you do then do it well and your clients will notice the difference and it will set your barn apart.

4. Treat it like a business, not a hobby.

One of the most difficult things for many people to do when they start a new business is to go from hobby to business owner. The transition can be hard and it might take a while but it is vital for a successful horse business. Many people underestimate how much everything changes when it becomes your sole income and the responsibility becomes heavy. Your clients will not understand this because they are not paying your bills or feeling the weight of responsibility that comes with owning your own business. Once you are able to make the transition and accept your new role as CEO of your barn, you will be pleasantly surprised at how much better you feel inside and with that will come a new confidence.

5. Don't go into extreme debt for your business.

Sometimes smaller is much better to start with. One of the biggest mistakes David and I made when we started our horse boarding business was that we borrowed too much money from the bank. We built too big to start and we didn't realize all the stress and pressure we would feel from the monthly business mortgage. You really do become a slave to the lender. I encourage you to start slow and grow as your business grows. You will be glad you did in the long run.

6. It's not personal, it's business.

Running a business can be difficult at times especially when you have to make a decision that is not popular with your clients. They might even take it personally especially if you have a friendship with them. Learning to make difficult choices and then taking the time to explain those choices to your clients is the best thing you can do. You will show them that you respect them enough to answer their questions and it will make them feel that they have value to you and your business.

You will not always win a popularity contest and you might even lose a client now and then but you have to do what is best for the business. If they are willing to ride the changes out with you, they might find that those changes have made your barn a much better place to be.

7. Treat your clients with respect under all circumstances (even when it is extremely hard).

I have failed at this a few times over the years. I have let my emotions get involved (and my temper) and treated a boarder in a non-professional way. The times that I have done this were my low points and the first thing I had to do was apologize for my behavior. We are human and we will all blow it. When we are the one that has made the mistake it is vital to learn to say, "I'm sorry." This is something that is so important and I guarantee that it will set you apart as a business owner and person.

8. Take time for yourself and rest!

Running a horse operation is a hard and very physical lifestyle. Don't burn yourself out. Take time to rest and play and get away if you can. It will refresh you in so many ways.

9. Surround yourself with positive and motivated people that share the same work ethic.

There are plenty of people in this world that will bring you down but if you want to work in an environment that is positive then you need to make a conscious decision to work with others that share the same values as yourself.

If you own a barn and need to hire help, then hire people that are going to work hard and be an asset to your place. Hire people that take pride in their work and in your barn. If you are a trainer then hire people that have the same passion and understand the importance of putting the horse first and not rushing to get the job done. If you hang around people all day that complain then soon you will find yourself complaining all day.

The job can be tough at times and we all have our moments when we complain but when you work with people that are positive then you will find yourself being positive most of the time.

If you are the owner of the business then you have the wonderful choice to decide who you are going to have work with you at your barn. It is easy to walk into a barn and tell what kind of place it is immediately. How the place is cared for and run says a lot about the owners. It doesn't matter if your barn is big or small, it doesn't cost money to keep a barn clean. It just takes hard work. Find people that are willing to work as hard as you and you will notice a big difference in your place.

10. Remember that your clients have a history before they came to you.

Your clients might need some time to adjust. Be patient. Every barn you walk into will operate a little differently. What is important at one place might not be an issue at another. Each barn will have a different set of rules and a different way of doing things.

When a new boarder comes to your barn they are going to need time to adjust. Be patient and be willing to explain things to them if they are doing things that are not permitted at your barn. Even if they read your barn rules they may need reminding at one time or another. The same would be true for trainers. When a new client comes in and they have trained under a different trainer for a long time, they are going to have to learn a few things differently. Each trainer does things differently and although the differences might be small they are still important.

Take time, be patient and above all else remember that some of the bad and unsafe habits your new client has might have been taught by a trainer that didn't know what they were doing. Be patient and wise in choosing your words to correct and be encouraging. Positive correction and encouragement will be one of the most important things you do when you come across an issue that needs to be addressed.

11. Consistency always wins.

My husband and I are very consistent in how we run our barn. To some it might sound extreme but to us it works and it works well. We treat our barn just like a job and that means that we get up each morning at the same time and start work at the same time. We feed and put our horses outside at the same time every day and bring them back in at the same time each evening.

We have cleaned our stalls at the same time each day for the last ten years. Our place works like clockwork and it runs smoothly and I believe the horses do much better when they know what to expect and our boarders have a comfort in knowing that there are no surprises. They know what to expect and it brings them a comfort that has contributed to our success.

If you find a system that works for you then keep it. You get to design your business any way you want and no matter how you run it, try to keep it as consistent as you can and your clients will appreciate it and you will find your job much easier.

12. Don't be afraid to work hard because you will worker harder at the beginning then you ever have before.

When I tell people that want to work for us that the work is hard and physical they always tell me "No problem they can handle it." Once they start working at our facility they always come to David or me and tell us they didn't realize that there was so much to do on a farm. It always surprises them.

Now as the barn owner get ready to double the work load! Remember as the owner your job doesn't end when you clock out for the day or the weekend and it definitely doesn't stop for holidays.

I am here to tell you that if you are ready for hard work and not afraid to work seven days a week (especially in the beginning of your new business) then you are on your way to success. Having a business is the hardest thing I have ever done but I can say it does get much easier and the hard work pays off. It just takes time. Don't give up and the days will get easier.

13. Learn from your mistakes and then move on.

I have sure made my share of mistakes over the years especially in the beginning. I made many mistakes purely on emotion and then I had to deal with the consequences of the mistakes. The best classroom you will ever have is right in your own barn.

You will learn more then you could imagine and when you make a mistake, learn from it and move on. Don't hang on to it because it will slow you down and cripple you. Learn to keep going and move forward.

Remember most of all-Every successful trainer, barn owner or anyone else that you know in the horse industry has made many mistakes along the path to success. We all do.

14. Try to learn something new every day. It will change your life.

The most successful people are not afraid to keep learning. They keep going to clinics and seminars and are not afraid to ask questions. Things are always changing and we are learning every day how to better take care of these beautiful horses on our farms. I encourage you to keep learning and try different things. You will grow on the inside when you are open to learning on a daily basis. Be ready for opportunities to learn and you will start to change in so many positive ways.

15. Don't let success scare you.

Once you get there enjoy it because you deserve it! Becoming a successful business doesn't happen overnight and it takes time and guts. Don't let others pull you down along the way and once you get to the point where your horse business has become successful, enjoy it. You have worked hard to get there and no one else will ever understand all that you sacrificed to make your dream a reality except your family and a few close friends.

Be proud of your accomplishments and take time to savor the journey. It has made you into a business person that is confident and secure in your decisions. The best and most rewarding part about success is ahead. Now you can share your road to success with others and help them gain the confidence they need to make it in the horse industry.

Chapter 55

Don't Be Intimidated By What Other Boarding Facilities Say They Offer

One of my favorite things to do is visit other horse boarding facilities. I love to walk through other barns and see how they are designed. There are some pretty amazing barns in our area and they are beautiful. It can be extremely intimidating when you walk through a barn and see all they have to offer. It can make you feel like your barn will never be as good if you allow it. Let me start off by saying, don't go there! Don't be intimidated by what other boarding facilities say they offer.

Before we built our barn and indoor arena, I drove around Wisconsin and toured many barns so I could get an idea of what I wanted our barn to look and feel like. Each barn I went to was unique and I appreciated all the differences. Each place had their own way of doing things and the little things they did set their place apart. It didn't matter to me if the barn was large or small, they were all special.

After we built our place and were open for boarding the real work began. With that came the chores and taking care of the horses and also the promotion and advertising of our place. Now that our sole income was coming from horse boarding and we had a huge business mortgage to pay I started to feel the pressure to make sure we were full and that we had the best amenities that we could offer.

Comparing to others

I started comparing our facility to others and what they offered. I quickly became insecure in what our barn offered and I started feeling like everyone else's place was far better than ours. The pressure to build "Bigger and better" was mounting up inside of me and I started putting that pressure on my husband.

Within the next two years I urged him to build a second larger outdoor arena and buy a large round pen. Money was extremely tight and we should have waited but I was convinced that those things would bring in more boarders. I started thinking about a cross-country course and jumps and it went on and on. Thank goodness he has more sense than me. He did build the arena and we bought a round pen but after that we stopped and I took a deep breath.

The other thing I would do often when we were a very young and growing business was to look at other barn websites and see what they offer for services. It was amazing to me what barns offered as part of the board and each place had their own marketing strategy to make their business stand out.

I read one website that offered in their board, daily check of every horse when they are being walked outside in the morning and walked back inside at dinner time. They offered "Personal care and hands on daily inspection." It was smart marketing and then I realized that I do the same thing here at our farm daily! I just didn't advertise it the way this other farm did.

I would become so intimidated in those early years and feel like we could never keep up with the other established barns in our area. I was missing the big picture and I had a lot to learn about business.

Years later I finally get it! It doesn't matter how big your place is or what you offer for amenities. If you run an honest place where the care of the horse is first and you do the things you say you are going to do, then the right clients will find you and they will stay.

Smaller is better for many

There are people out there that are looking for a smaller place and prefer a quieter atmosphere. They don't need a jump course or five outdoor arenas. They are content to spend time riding and enjoying their horse and your place will be perfect for them. There are also people who love a busy barn with lots of activity and many options for riding and if you own a large facility then you will find your clientele also.

The one thing I have learned over the years is that there are plenty of people who own horses and your place no matter the size will be perfect for many of them. They just need to find you. Don't be intimidated by other barns and what they say they offer. Instead take what you do offer at your barn and promote it.

If you are small barn then advertise all the advantages of a nice quiet place and the individual care that goes with a smaller barn. Smaller barns have so many great advantages but many times the barn owner doesn't realize it because they are stuck. They can't get past what they *don't have*. Smaller barns have so many wonderful qualities and they are a huge asset to the horse industry.

Remember, there is always going to be a fancier barn with more amenities no matter what size your place is. There is always going to be a barn that seems perfect on the outside but remember that the size of the building is not what makes a barn great or successful. It is the people inside and the people running the place that make the difference and set the barn apart.

Remember that the size of the building is not what makes a barn great or successful. It is the people inside and the people running the place that make the difference and set the barn apart.

When it comes down to it, all anyone really wants is a place where their horse will be taken care of and they don't have to worry. You could have the nicest barn in your area with all the amenities imaginable but if the care is terrible and horses seem stressed then all those other things don't matter at all.

You will find the right clients

There are many different types of riders and disciplines and you will find the right clients for your place. Our place is large and we have a busy barn. There are many people who love the busyness of our facility. We have also had people come to our barn and leave a few months later because our place was too busy for them. They didn't like to ride with so many other people in the arena. I totally respect that and even though I was disappointed that they left, I was happy that they found the right place for their needs.

I encourage you today to start thinking about all the wonderful things your barn offers and stop comparing your place to other barns. Take what you have and go with it. If you can add things on later that is great. Just don't do what I did early on when I put pressure on myself and everyone around me to have it all at once. I am so glad those days are long behind me. I am so much happier now and you will be too.

Chapter 56

During Sickness and in Health

They say the true test of someone's character will come out during times in their life when things do not go as planned. I believe that is so very true and that will spill over into your business life just the same.

Running a horse business will bring many challenges along the way but one of the more difficult ones will be when an emergency or illness hits the barn. How you handle it is crucial to how your boarders will respond.

I was talking to a man the other day that had the unfortunate bad luck of having a contagious virus run through one of his barns. A handful of horses were very sick and had fevers. The veterinarian came out immediately and this barn owner did everything according to what the doctors advised to isolate the virus. He told me that in his state there was no mandatory quarantine for the type of virus his barn was dealing with and it would be his decision as the barn owner whether or not to quarantine the barn.

He had never dealt with this before and panic started to run through his barn. He had boarders that threatened to move their horse if he didn't quarantine the barn immediately. He also had boarders that wanted to go to horse shows and they threatened to move their horses if he did quarantine the barn.

It was truly a nightmare coming true for this barn owner. There was a lot riding on the line and of course income was a big part of it. He also had his reputation at stake.

His barn was a fairly new boarding facility and if he let these horses leave the property for a show, he would hear about it from one group of boarders. He knew there would be people out there who would feel he was irresponsible for letting any horses off his property while there were sick horses. He was extremely worried about the ramifications on both sides and then of course there is social media where so many people put everything out there for all to see even when they don't have all the facts.

He had to make a decision fast and he was going to need to stand by his decision no matter the outcome. I talked with this man and told him that he would get through this but first he needed to make a decision on what he was going to do.

A leader overnight

This barn owner became a leader overnight and wrote a very well written letter informing all his clients why he was going to quarantine the barn. He covered everything in the letter including his communication with the veterinarians involved and told his boarders that this was how it was going to be done.

I talked with this man and told him that even though this situation was so very unfortunate, I believe it transformed him into a strong and confident business person that day.

No one wants a virus to run through their barn but if you are in the business long enough there is a good chance that it might happen. Horses are no different than people, they catch things and then they spread them.

This barn owner grew more as a leader and barn manager in a few short weeks than most of us grow over a couple of years. He had no choice but to take control of the chaos that was happening at his barn.

Life is good when the sun is out

Any job is easy when the sun is out and the weather is perfect. We all love our barns when the horses are out on pasture enjoying the warm sun and our clients tell us that we have the best facility in the world. It doesn't get any easier than that.

As a barn owner you will experience many different types of clients. I want to remind you that even when tragedy strikes and panic hits the barn your clients are going to be looking for someone to lead and take control. If you don't do it, then you will have chaos.

They might not like the decisions you make regarding a difficult situation and you might even lose a boarder or two that do not agree with you. That is okay. At the end of the day you need to do what is best for your barn as a whole, not just what is best for one or two pushy people that know how to get under your skin.

One day at a time

Take each situation as it arises one day at a time and surround yourself with people who can offer sound advice and help you through the tough decisions you might need to make.

Remember that each experience will make you stronger and more confident after it is over. We don't learn when everything is easy. We learn when adversity comes and we need to make choices.

You will get through it and one day you will be able to help another person that is going through the same thing. Some of your clients may not stay at your barn through sickness and in health but as barn owners we are there for the long haul and that means taking the bad with the good.

Don't worry the good days are always just around the corner.

Chapter 57

Okay, So You Made a Poor Decision

We all have the best intentions but the truth is we are going to make mistakes and poor decisions that we need to recover from. I have been there so many times during my career of working in the horse industry. It is how you deal with it afterwards that will make the difference in your business.

Starting and running a business is extremely hard and dealing with animals is even harder because they can't tell you what is wrong or why they don't get along with each other. They won't tell you who tore the fence down or who kicked who out in the paddock.

It sounded good at the time

All your decisions that are made at your barn will directly relate to the horses in your care and some of them might seem like great ideas at the time and then after you make the change you quickly realize it was a bad decision. It is bound to happen the longer you are working around horses and people and when it does you need to own up to it and move forward. Sometimes the best way to learn what is going to work or not work is to just try it.

I have made poor decisions on where to place a horse in a herd and I have made poor decisions when it comes to dealing with my boarders. It has been a journey of trials and errors but through them I have grown into a more confident horse professional and with each experience both good and bad came some earned wisdom.

Wisdom doesn't come when life is easy and your barn never has any issues. It comes through adversity and from that comes character and strength. How you handle it after you made the mistake or poor decision will show what kind of leader you are and your clients will see that.

Wisdom doesn't come when life is easy and your barn never has any issues. It comes through adversity and from that comes character and strength.

Get a second opinion

Running a horse business in not easy and you are going to make many decisions every day. Take them as they come and if you are not sure what to do when a problem arises then I encourage you to talk with someone in the business that can walk you through it and give you a second opinion. Find a person that has been in the business longer and who has a reputation for being positive and honest.

There are plenty of people out there that will complain about everything and a year later they are still complaining about the same things. Don't waste your time getting advice from someone that doesn't want to learn and grow. They will only bring you down.

Okay, so you made a poor decision. Learn from it, move on and don't do it again. If your clients know that your heart was in the right place but you just made a mistake they will be more understanding then you would ever guess.

The early years of any new business are going to be filled with many good decisions and bad decisions. As time goes by your good decisions will strongly outnumber your bad ones and eventually your mistakes will become fewer and smaller. When this happens you will know that you are growing as a business owner and person.

Chapter 58

Creating a Team at Your Barn

Creating a team of employees or a committed team of clients is something that every barn owner should strive for. I am so glad that we have a wonderful team at our barn that I know I can depend on anytime to help at our farm. Finding people that take ownership in your barn and help create a positive atmosphere is a sign of a strong and healthy business. When you find a team of people that are dedicated to you and the barn, it doesn't get any better than that.

David and I do most of the work at our barn but we do have boarders that come and clean stalls with us on Saturdays. They love it and I am glad because by Saturday I am pretty burned out and both David and I could use the rest. These people come and clean and take pride in their work and I don't have to worry about a thing. When they are done the stalls are cleaned and bedded and the water buckets are all topped off. It is a wonderful feeling.

They are valuable

Whether you have full time employees or a handful of boarders cleaning on Saturdays, they are both equally important and valuable to you and the success of your barn. The most positive way to create a team is to let them know how valuable they are.

I feel like our entire barn is a family and I also feel they are a team that takes care of each other and watch's out for each other's horses. They are very protective of each other and the horses at the farm and they are the first to call me if they see someone strange drive into the farm and something doesn't seem right. The support system is amazing.

Creating a team of people that take ownership in your barn takes time and personal investment on your part. Get to know the clients at your barn and allow them to get to know you. Once they see how you run the place on a daily basis and how much you care they will start to climb aboard. When they see that you run a barn with honesty and integrity, they will want to be part of it and nothing less will do.

When you get to the point where your clients have taken ownership in your barn then you have created a team and a family and that makes for a very successful barn. That is when you know you are doing something right and it will set your barn apart.

You need to nurture it

I have had so many people over the years come to board at our barn and they can't believe the support system that is in place due to the care of the boarders for each other and their horses. Creating this kind of support and unity amongst boarders doesn't just happen by chance. As the barn owner you need to nurture it and encourage it to grow and once it takes root, it will take off and you will feel success in a completely new way.

Remember that behind every successful barn there is a great team of employees and clients and they are both valuable beyond measure. Don't ever take them for granted!

Chapter 59

Take the High Road-Even When it is Difficult to Do

If you have decided that owning and managing your own horse business is what you want to do for a career then I applaud you. Then I encourage you to take it one day at a time and make sure you surround yourself with positive people who will help you through the tough days.

You are going to have days when you feel like nothing is going right and your clients are not happy with you. Those days will pass and the sun will come out again, but I would like to give you some advice if I may.

As long as you are in business there is going to come a time when you and a client will not agree on something and they will become upset with you. It might be because of a miscommunication about the care of their horse or it could be because you made a mistake and they are not ready to forgive and let it go.

Whatever the reason that you and a client are having a problem, I encourage you to take the high road and treat them and their horse the best you can and even if they move (which many times they do) don't be the one doing the talking or the bad mouthing.

Keep it professional and even if they shoot off their mouth, eventually it will die down and people will see the truth just by how you run your barn on a daily basis.

Don't give them the power

I know it can be very hard to take the high road and forgive the other person but once you do this, you will feel the weight lifted off your shoulders and they will not control your day and how it is going to go. Don't give them the power.

I have been hurt many times over the years from clients whom I thought were happy and were my friends and then something happens and they change in a moment. I have been sent ugly emails and had things written on Facebook that were very upsetting. When this happened I became so upset and I didn't know what to do, so I took some time to pray about it and decided not to respond at all unless it was with positive words.

In the long run each difficult experience I have had has only helped me grow as a person and hopefully it has made be a better human being.

Running a business of any kind means that you will be in the leadership position and that will not always be the popular place to be especially when you need to enforce the rules of your barn. It doesn't always set well with some clients and those are the ones that usually move on and then they have the same issues at the next place.

Don't take it personally. It happens to all of us and as long as you are doing the best job you can do and are taking great care to make sure the horses are safe, happy and healthy at your barn then you are doing great.

Take the high road and you will never regret it.

Chapter 60

Can You Make a Living At Boarding Horses?

One of the most frequently asked questions I get is-how did we know if we could make a living at boarding horses? I wish I could say it was an easy answer but it took us some time to really get a grasp on what our income would be and if we could make an honest living boarding horses. There is so much that goes in to the whole equation of starting a business and boarding horses and it is no different from any other start-up business.

One of the main reasons I wrote my first book, "What it really takes to start and run a horse business" is because I realized that there weren't any other books on how to get started and I mean starting from empty farmland. Starting from the very beginnings of new construction and all that goes with it was a much bigger undertaking then I ever dreamed.

Getting a business up and going and especially a business dealing with animals takes time and an extreme amount of preparation. We went through the process of figuring out a business plan (which I recommend to anyone that is going into business) and putting numbers together and the entire process took two years before we ever started construction. Even after we started building our barn, new costs and surprises were popping up every day.

Yes you can!

There are many people who will tell you that you can't make a living at boarding horses but I am here to say that you can. You just need to be disciplined and very smart about it and very conservative in the early stages.

Many people fall in love with the idea of boarding horses for many different reasons but many of them do not do their homework to find out how much everything will cost to run their farm through all four seasons. Even the change of seasons will bring different expenses.

I am going to be very honest and tell you that I had rose colored glasses on myself. I thought it was going to be so much easier than it was and after I had added up all the numbers for income each month I thought we were going to have plenty of money after all the bills were paid. That was not the case.

One of the biggest misconceptions people have about our farm is that they think we are making all kinds of money. They see our barn and the number of horses we have on the property and what we charge for board and they add it all up. What they don't realize at all is the expense to run the farm and the mortgage. They don't know what our hay cost for the year or insurance or even electricity. The people who do ask are always a little in shock when I tell them what our monthly bills are to keep the place going. I do believe that if I can be honest and help someone who wants to get into the business, it can only help them start out much better than we did.

A realistic view

Figuring out what to charge for board and then estimating your monthly expenses can take a couple of years to really have a realistic view of income coming in and expenses going out. Those early years are critical to being successful and that is when you need to be the most conservative.

I always tell people slow and steady always wins. It might not be fun at the time but it is very important for good business decisions. Now many years later I encourage people to write up a business plan whether you need to borrow money or not. You will see things in your business that you never even thought of before. Most people think that you only need to prepare a business plan if you need to borrow money but that is not true. Do it for yourself.

Preparing a business plan will be the smartest thing you do in those early stages. Starting your horse business off on the right foot with a solid foundation is so much easier than finding out a year later that you are losing money and everything is costing so much more than you estimated.

Learning to run a business is one thing but it is extremely hard to run a business if you have to work a second job on top of it. We did that for many years because of the mistakes we made in the beginning and it will wear you down very fast. I encourage you to take some time see what it really takes to start and run a horse business. Do your homework and ask questions. It will pay off in the long run.

Chapter 61

Don't Give Up, the Days Will Get Easier

Having your own horse business is a great life but as you can see horse barn management is about so much more than feeding horses and cleaning stalls. It is about so much more than daily horse care.

I truly believe it takes a couple of years to fully get a grasp of running a business and how to do it right. You will grow as you learn from the daily job of running your barn and your people skills will grow also.

Your clients will change a lot in the early years but new people and new horses will arrive and your business will grow with each change. Before you know it your boarders will stay longer and your turnover will become much less. The days will become consistent and the job will become much easier.

I have talked with many people over the last couple of years that become so frustrated and want to quit and sell their farm. They are tired of dealing with people and fixing everything that gets broken on their farm. It is a reality that people can be hard to deal with now and then and horses will break everything they can, but if you stick it out I promise you it will become easier. It will mean changing as you grow and making decisions that are better for you and your family but may not be popular with your boarders. That is all part of it and you will get to that point if you want to succeed.

You need to do what is best for you

You need to remember that your boarders will come and go but you will still be there on the farm so you need to do what is best for you as the barn owner. You can change things now and then to help a client but you will learn to know when to draw the line in the sand and say enough is enough and you will be relieved that you did. It is all part of becoming a business owner.

You are one of the privileged few that get to walk out to your office each morning and hear nickers waiting for you. You are living the dream that so many others would love to have. Embrace your position as CEO of your barn and learn from each situation that you are faced with and watch your business grow and flourish.

What a great life to be able to care for these amazing horses we love so much. I wish you the very best at your barn and may all your days be filled with nickers and happy horses.

God bless you and your horse business.

Sheri Grunska

Made in the USA
Middletown, DE
07 September 2020